NINETEENTH CENTUR✍ **W9-CTH-817**

DISCOVERING ART SERIES

Nineteenth Century Art

adapted by Ariane Ruskin

Foreword by Howard Conant, Ed.D.
New York University

McGRAW-HILL BOOK COMPANY

New York • San Francisco • Toronto

Also in paperback in the Discovering Art Series:

GREEK & ROMAN ART,
adapted by Ariane Ruskin and Michael Batterberry
CHINESE & ORIENTAL ART, adapted by Michael
Batterberry
TWENTIETH CENTURY ART, by Michael Batterberry

In hardcover:

CHINESE & ORIENTAL ART, adapted by Michael
Batterberry
GREEK & ROMAN ART, adapted by Ariane Ruskin and
Michael Batterberry
NINETEENTH CENTURY ART, adapted by Ariane Ruskin
SEVENTEENTH & EIGHTEENTH CENTURY ART, adapted
by Ariane Ruskin
TWENTIETH CENTURY ART, by Michael Batterberry
ART OF THE EARLY RENAISSANCE, adapted by Michael
Batterberry
ART OF THE HIGH RENAISSANCE, adapted by Ariane
Ruskin
PREHISTORIC ART AND ANCIENT ART OF THE NEAR
EAST, adapted by Ariane Ruskin
ART OF THE MIDDLE AGES, adapted by Michael
Batterberry
PRIMITIVE ART, adapted by Ariane Ruskin and Michael
Batterberry

Acknowledgment is hereby given to **Purnell & Sons Ltd** for the right to base this
work on the text of the magazine series "Discovering Art" and to Fratelli Fabbri
Editori for the right to make adaptations from the Italian text of *Capolavori Nei
Secoli.*

NINETEENTH CENTURY ART
Illustrations copyright © 1961-1964, 1968, 1973 by Fratelli Fabbri
Editori, Milan, Italy. No part of this work may be reproduced without
the permission of the publisher.

Library of Congress Catalog Card Number: 68-55273

FOREWORD

by Howard Conant

Professor and Chairman, Department of Art Education; and Head, Division of Creative Arts, New York University

THE PUBLICATION of Ariane Ruskin's *Nineteenth Century Art* is an event of unusual cultural and educational importance. It is one of the first art histories for young readers to deal exclusively, comprehensively, and incisively with the complex century preceding our own. And it is one of the first written in a style which can be easily understood by a youthful audience, but which does not sacrifice any of the scholarly depth that adult readers demand.

For these reasons, Miss Ruskin's book is well-suited as a reference text for use in upper elementary and secondary school art and social studies curricula. And in conjunction with other volumes in the "Discovering Art Series," *Nineteenth Century Art* would serve ideally as text material for rapidly emerging secondary school and junior college programs of study in the humanities.

Librarians who have long been aware of the lack of nineteenth century art history material, particularly that which deals with cultural developments of the early eighteen hundreds, will find this volume invaluable as a general reference. They will also welcome Miss Ruskin's encyclopedic, but never superficial, coverage of the art and artists of this critical period. Teachers of art and related subjects, such as literature, music, and social studies, will be pleased, indeed surprised, to find that *Nineteenth Century Art* is a text for which they need make no apologies to their students. Unlike many art histories, which often are little more than dreary descriptions of bygone periods, Miss Ruskin's work possesses insight, forthrightness, and commitment. Her vivid, penetrating analysis of nineteenth-century culture simultaneously clears the atmosphere of vague remembrances and brings to life the artists and art works of this vibrant and exciting age.

Teachers and librarians will also be pleased to find that Miss Ruskin consistently maintains a level of scholarly depth which is 5 appealing to an adult audience. She has skillfully expressed advanced theoretical concepts in language which can be understood by youthful readers, but has not sacrificed the element of challenge to adults.

Nineteenth Century Art is rich in details, including relevant biographical, historical, and sociological data which will help readers place artists and their works into appropriate historical, philosophical, artistic, and social contexts. The author's penetrating revelation of the personalities of individual artists and her clear-cut aesthetic evaluations of the works of art which they created will contribute significantly to a better understanding of the nature of nineteenth-century culture and the persons who contributed to its development.

Many people today, including students in secondary school, know all too little about art history and aesthetics. Elementary school art education is often limited to creating or copying things with paints, pencils, paper, or clay. For a number of reasons, elementary school art students do not develop an understanding of the world's art heritage. And even though social science textbooks are occasionally illustrated with works of art, authors and teachers rarely do more than *use* the art to illustrate the characteristics of various historical periods. Contributing further to this situation is the condition of art education in many secondary schools and colleges, where students receive no more than a flash survey of art history. Unfortunately, all this adds up to produce adults, unsure of their knowledge and unsure of their taste, who will tap their foreheads when confronted with an actual work of art and ask: "Let's see . . . is that by Cézanne or Degas?—or maybe Monet?" This is much sadder than: "I don't know anything about art, but I know what I like!"

By now it must be apparent that the only present solution to the problem of educational "gaposis" in art is self-education. A person today must decide between art-educating himself or remaining artistically and culturally illiterate. Books of the quality of this volume are absolutely essential to one's education in art; and even if an individual should receive a thorough art history education as part of his schooling, competent texts and reference materials are essential.

Miss Ruskin has done as much as any author could do, and much more than most art historians have, in attempting to fill a portion of the art education gap. And she has performed this task with skill and candor, which is important because today's alert readers, young and old, demand quality and integrity in every piece of reading matter which comes into their hands. They have learned to reject inferior material—not only poor fiction, but superficial texts and pseudo-scholarly nonfiction as well. In my judgment, Miss Ruskin's *Nineteenth Century Art* will not only meet their rigorous standards, but provide unexpected dividends as well. Perhaps the most important of these will be the realization that the condition of human life can be richly enhanced by the development of a deep and lasting knowledge of art and the artists who created it.

CONTENTS

Foreword   5

Introduction   11

Neoclassicism   14

Romanticism   42

Realism and the Pre-Raphaelites   98

Impressionism   135

*The Postimpressionists and the End of
the Nineteenth Century*   180

List of Illustrations   245

Index   250

Introduction

LET US examine closely a painting considered great at the opening of the nineteenth century. The *Coronation of Napoleon and Josephine* (Plate 1) by Jacques Louis David (1748-1825) would be a good example. The coronation took place on December 2, 1804, in the Cathedral of Notre Dame de Paris. It was elaborately staged and prepared. David was installed in a box from which he viewed the ceremony and made numerous drawings, but the final picture was far from an exact portrayal of the event. Originally David had intended to depict Napoleon crowning himself after he had seized the crown from the Pope, but he was persuaded that this was unwise and changed his picture to a benign image of Napoleon crowning the Empress Josephine. The canvas was so huge that the old church of Cluny became David's studio, and the various dignitaries present at the ceremony came there to pose for the painting.

Now let us look at a work characteristic of the latter part of that same century, a picture still considered great today. *The Gare St.-Lazare* (Plate 2) by Claude Monet (1840–1926) is such a work. An extraordinary change in the technique of painting seems to have taken place. Seen close at hand, the picture seems no more than a series of daubs and splashes of paint. At some distance, the human eye itself brings the canvas into focus, and a cavernous railway station, clouds of smoke dispersing in the damp gray atmosphere, comes into view. Monet was a member of a group of painters known as "impressionists."

Were it not for the dress of the figures, it would take a practiced eye to tell that the *Coronation of Napoleon and Josephine* had not been painted by some master of the seventeenth or even sixteenth century. Why, then, does it differ so violently from *The Gare St.-Lazare,* painted less than a century later? What is the explanation for the truly amazing revolution which took place in all the visual arts during the short space of a hundred years?

1. *Coronation of Napoleon and Josephine* (detail), by Jacques Louis David

In the nineteenth century, as in the century that preceded it, the world looked to France for leadership in art, and it was in France that the revolution took place. As with all revolutions, there were many contributing factors, and in this case all the

2. *The Gare St.-Lazare,*
by Claude Monet

factors tended in one way or another to lead to impressionism, which led to the final break with traditional representation that characterizes today's art. An interesting story unfolds if we study the various movements in nineteenth-century art one by one. 13

Neoclassicism

AT THE turn of the nineteenth century France had just undergone a revolution that was political, not artistic, one of the most shattering in human history. The lavish Court of Louis XVI—the Court of France which had employed the most skilled artists, holding sway over European tastes and manners for more than a century—had come crashing down, its king and queen executed, its members driven into exile or guillotined. The revolutionaries were intent on stamping out every trace of their former rulers. Nothing was to remain the same. There were twelve new months, with names such as Gérminal and Floréal, each divided into three weeks of ten days, and a new deity, a goddess of wisdom, was installed in the Cathedral of Notre Dame.

Men gave up the knee breeches and silk stockings of the *ancien régime* (literally "the old rule") in favor of loose ankle-length trousers, and women discarded their ample skirts, nipped waists, and flounces for slender, draped, high-waisted garments that were meant to make them look like matrons of the ancient Roman Republic, which the new republic was to resemble in every possible way. Powdered wigs were never seen again; the "Psyche knot" and Brutus haircut took their place.

There was another reason for the new fascination with all things characteristic of ancient Rome and Greece. Since the time of the Renaissance, fragments of ancient sculpture had been unearthed from time to time in Rome and elsewhere, but it was not until the eighteenth century that serious excavations got under way. In 1719 Prince Elbeuf, in search of crushed marble near Naples, was told by peasants of some pits from which whole statues had been extracted. When the area was inspected, it turned out to be the site of ancient Herculaneum, buried along with Pompeii by the great eruption of Vesuvius in A.D. 79. In 1735 diggings were undertaken at Herculaneum, and they yielded not only superb classical statues in a perfect state of preservation, but also Roman wall paintings such as modern Europe had never seen—

subjects like Theseus after his slaying of the Minotaur, Chiron teaching Achilles to play the lyre, or Hercules finding the infant Telephus being suckled by a doe, all elegantly executed, with colors almost as fresh as the day they were painted. By the middle of the century Pompeii had also been discovered, and two entire cities, full of a wealth of classical decoration, were coming to the eyes of Europe, standing as they were, untouched since the day the fearful fiery cloud of ash and lava had settled upon them. Meanwhile, travelers were more and more often visiting Athens and viewing the crumbling but unburied remains of Greek art, from which the Roman works had drawn their inspiration, and from which they were often copied. The drawings of James Stuart and Nicholas Revett brought the beauty of the Parthenon, partially destroyed in 1687, to the attention of the rest of Europe, and the Earl of Elgin, moved by the desire to bring the glory of Greece to his native land, simply seized its principal statuary and sent it to England. Thus, the first remnants of the work of the greatest sculptor of the Golden Age of Greece, Phidias, were to be seen in London.

In 1764 Johann J. Winckelmann published his great *History of Ancient Art,* and laid the foundation for the whole movement of neoclassicism, the "new Classicism." Winckelmann was the first art historian to see his subject not merely as a sequence of artists' schools and works, but as one aspect of the evolution of human thought. The styles of various works of art, he felt, not only indicate the personal manner of individual artists, but reflect the philosophy, the general tenor, of a whole civilization. His advice to the artist was quite simple: "To take the ancients for models is our only way to become great, yes, unsurpassable if we can." He felt that the Greek artists' frequent opportunities to observe the human body, in the gymnasium and the games, had caused them to

form general concepts of beauty for the individual parts of the body as well as for its proportions: concepts that were meant to rise above nature, being taken from a spiritual realm that existed only in the mind.

I believe that imitating the Greeks can teach us to become wise more quickly, since in their works we find not only the essence of whatever is beautiful throughout nature but also the extent to which even the highest form of natural beauty can be wisely and boldly transcended.

The ancient concepts of the unity and perfection of nature will clarify our concepts of nature in its diversity. The artist will discover the beauty of nature and combine it with beauty in the absolute; the constant presence of the noble forms of Greek art will help him to find his own rules.

Even if the imitation of nature could give the artist everything else, it would not yield him the essential truth of forms. That he can acquire only from the Greeks. In the statuary of the Greeks all aspects of natural and ideal beauty are merged and defined by the most noble of contours; or rather, this contour represents the highest concept of both.

Finally, the most prominent general characteristic of the Greek masterpieces is a noble simplicity and silent greatness in pose as well as in expression. As the depths of the sea remain always at rest however the surface may be agitated, so the expression in the figures of the Greeks reveals in the midst of passion a great and steadfast soul.

As there was already considerable interest in the works of classical antiquity, Winckelmann's ideas were received with enthusiasm.

With wave after wave of revolution and the rise of Napoleon as protector of France against foreign invading armies, the First Republic gave way to the First Empire. But, in the realm of dress, architecture, and art generally, Napoleon's empire was to be a Roman empire, just as the republic it succeeded had been a Roman republic. Napoleon donned the laurel crown of the Caesars and a new school of artists was called into existence. At its head was the already famous Jacques Louis David.

In his youth, before the fall of the *ancien régime,* David had won a prize enabling him to study art in Rome. There he remained for five years, and the experience profoundly marked his painting. When he returned, he was fully a member of the school devoted to the ideas of Winckelmann and "neoclassicism," which drew its inspiration, as we have seen, from the wall paintings and sculpture so recently unearthed, thus favoring hard, sharp lines and figures as narrowly shadowed as those of a classical relief, ideal in feature, and apparently frozen for all time into the heroic and usually frontal poses typical of much of Roman and Greek statuary. David brushed aside the frivolity of court painting, of eighteenth-century life altogether, with deliberate disapproval. Moreover, he fitted his deeds to his artistic concept of life and set about undermining in any way possible the *ancien régime.* He sympathized wholeheartedly with the Revolution, which was just brewing on his return, and if it could be said to have had an official painter, David was that man.

He returned to Paris in 1781, and was made a member of the Academy, the official society of fine arts in France, the following year. But in 1784 he returned to Rome in order to paint the *Oath of the Horatii,* which was his first major success, and which marked the achievement of his mature style. He took his subject from the play by the great classical dramatist of the previous century, Corneille, but quickly returned to Corneille's source in antiquity, the account by the Roman historian Livy of the combat fought by representatives of the Romans and of their enemies, the Albans, in order to avoid a full-scale conflict. The Roman warriors, the Horatii, were triplet brothers, as were their opponents, the Curatii. Of the six, only one of the Horatii survived. On his return he discovered his sister, wife of one of the slain Curatii, mourning her husband. Angered that she placed her personal grief above the safety of the state, he slew her on the spot. David chose to paint the moment before battle when the three sons swear to their father on their swords to fight to the death for their country. The picture caused a sensation when it was exhibited. It is easy to appreciate the purely artistic reasons for the painting's success, but since then it has often been thought that this moral subject was also intended as a comment on contemporary politics, that the picture attracted attention as a pre-Revolution attack on the monarchy. It is, in fact, difficult to tell how much David himself saw his work as political.

But there can be no doubt about the political intent of his painting of *Brutus and His Dead Son*. It was exhibited at the Salon of 1789, the annual exhibition of paintings held by the Society of French Artists. This was in the early days of the Revolution, while the monarchy was still in existence, and the applicability of the picture's moral was so evident that Royalists made attempts to suppress the work. Brutus, like the survivor of the Horatii, put his country before his personal happiness, and he sentenced his own sons to death for treachery. The subject was immediately understood as a lesson for the king, who had signally failed to follow this noble example. For the picture, David had pursued archaeological accuracy to the point of having replicas of Roman furniture made for him.

During the Revolution David became a deputy and voted for the death of the king. He was placed in charge of fine arts for the Revolutionary government, organized pageants, abolished the Academy, and assisted in the foundation of the Institute which replaced it. He followed up his Roman subjects now with subjects taken from the Revolution. The *Oath of the Tennis Court,* in which he treated that recent event in modern dress according to the principles of his earlier paintings, was never completed. But with his three memorial portraits of the martyrs of the Revolution he created a new type of heroic composition. In the greatest of these, the *Death of Marat* (Plate 3), he portrayed Marat, a complicated man, part patriot and part scandalmonger, who was stabbed in his medicinal bath while busily penning attacks on his enemies, with all the austere grandeur of a departed Roman senator. By contrast, his brief pen sketches of the victims of the Revolution on the way to the guillotine tell a truer story. His penetrating record of Marie Antoinette in the tumbril, wizened and thin-lipped, is stark and pitiless. Thus he disposed of the favorite model of painters of an earlier school in a few telling lines.

David's first hero, Robespierre, the arid and sinister demagogue who managed to bring about the execution of everyone who opposed his rise to power, was eventually put to death, and the painter himself was consequently flung into prison. At this point

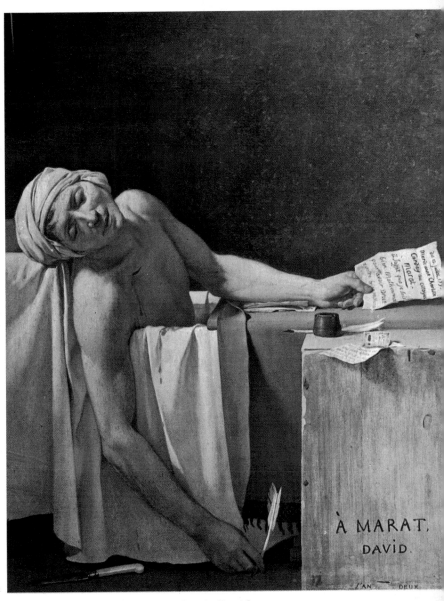

3. *Death of Marat*, by Jacques Louis David

his former wife, Charlotte Pécoul, who had divorced him because of his revolutionary activities, flew to his defense and campaigned vigorously for his release. He remarried her, and painted *The Sabine Women* (Plate 4) in honor of female heroism.

The women of the Sabine tribe are seen defending themselves against the Romans, who eventually carried them off as wives. There could not be a better example of David's early classical style. The scene is one of turmoil, but there is no action. Each figure appears separately chiseled in marble and heavily tinted with color. And yet, like classical statuary, the forms have a splendid grace and grandeur, even if we do not believe for a minute that either of the hearty warriors in the foreground would consider dealing his opponent a deathblow. It is all very decorative make-believe, neat and smoothly finished.

David could not survive long without a political hero. In 1798 he met Napoleon, and for the next seventeen years his painting ardently portrayed the cult of the Emperor. Perhaps the most important of his works of this period is the *Coronation of Napoleon and Josephine,* which we have already seen. To this scene of contemporary splendor David brought the same laws of classical composition he had employed in *The Sabine Women.* But whereas *The Sabine Women* was conceived in an antique mold, with bodies and heads idealized and impersonal, here David was obliged to display a hundred specific dignitaries as they actually looked, and his genius for portraiture, seen earlier in his sketches of unfortunates on their way to the guillotine, is spectacularly revealed. The figures, except for that of Napoleon himself, are all too human — some bored, some interested, some dignified, some merely themselves. Moreover, the work is far more relaxed than his earlier pictures, the outlines less pronounced, the light softer, the color richer.

The air of authority which led David to dominate a whole generation of younger painters is summed up in his pronouncement "the real patriot must be anxious to seize every means of enlightening his fellow citizens and put before their eyes the noble aspect of heroism and virtue." Unhappily, these beliefs led to the final disaster of his life. When Napoleon was defeated, David

4. *The Sabine Women,* **by Jacques Louis David**

went into exile in Brussels, where he died in 1825, like a Roman.

The styles of David's pupils were formed by their various reactions to the inspiration of the Napoleonic era. Some commemorated Napoleon's campaigns in a heroic, dramatic style which stirred the popular imagination, inspiring it to greater devotion and sacrifice, in accordance with David's exhortation. Napoleon himself, however, favored a crisp, smooth, and correct classicism. The artists who were foremost in gratifying the double nature of the Emperor's requirements and the popular imagination were two of David's followers: Baron François Gerard (1770–1837), who was responsible for a "sentimental" classicism, and

21

Baron Antoine Jean Gros (1771–1835), who created the heroic epic.

Gérard's style, as we can see from his *Cupid and Psyche* (Plate 5), inclined to sentimental prettiness. Cupid, the son of Venus, awakens the affection of his love, Psyche, whose name is very simply the Greek word for "mind." Again it is a subject for a Roman relief or wall painting, but it is handled with more emotionalism than the ancients would have thought suitable. Gérard's technique was more uniform than that of David, who frequently adjusted his brushwork to the nature of the subject so that it possessed a more living, flexible quality, as in the portrait of Mme. Récamier. Gérard, on the other hand, took pains to conceal individual brushstrokes in a smooth enamellike surface, where light and shade merge imperceptibly. He delighted in a clear, bright use of color much like the delicate brilliance of porcelain decoration. This "perfect" finish was highly prized throughout the nineteenth century.

Baron Antoine Jean Gros suited his epics to the grandeur of Napoleon's achievements, but was so carried away with emotion that he fairly burst the bonds of David's strict classicism. Although the almost theatrical classical gesture is not lacking, his canvases are full of color and very genuine movement. He had, in fact, a strong streak of the romantic in his work, yet his loyalty to the stylistic discipline of his master resulted in a conflict that tormented his life and led to his eventual suicide.

Among the first of his Napoleonic masterpieces was the *Pesthouse at Jaffa* (Plate 6), painted in 1804. Here Gros is still very close to David, and his design is one of simple classical frontality, yet the composition is made poignant by the large but languid figure in the foreground who tries in vain to rise to his feet. The picture is also a superb piece of political propaganda: As the Emperor prods a victim's chest with his ungloved hand, Gros suggests both his bravery and a kind of divine immunity to the danger of contagious disease.

Gros's painting of *The Battle of Nazareth* (Plate 7), heralds a dramatic change. Instead of the static composition of the Jaffa plague scene, we see now forms that eddy and surge across the

5. *Cupid and Psyche,* by Baron François Gérard

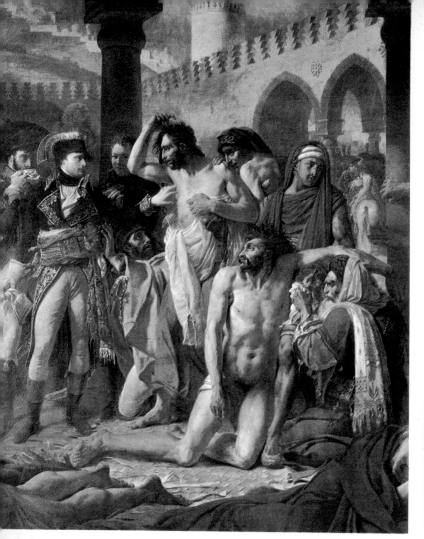

6. *Pesthouse at Jaffa,* **by Baron Antoine Jean Gros**

canvas like the uncertain tides of battle. In this canvas, depicting
the spectacular exploit in which 500 French troops defeated 6,000
Turks, there is no moment of classical calm whatever. Forms of
eruptive motion are merely suggested and enveloped in clouds of
gun smoke, shapes emerge and disappear, and touches of vermil-
lion carry the eye into the farthest distance. The color not only
is a part of the composition but makes us sense the magnitude of

7. *The Battle of Nazareth,* **by Baron Antoine Jean Gros**

the slaughter. This particular painting of Gros's is very near the great works of the romantic movement, which was directly opposed to classicism, as we shall see.

There were other contemporaries of equal caliber. Pierre-Paul Prud'hon, who painted the Empress Josephine (Plate 8, was known for the freer, more poetic atmosphere of his paintings, the silvery shadows of his backgrounds, and his pallid and creamy 25

8. *Portrait of the Empress Josephine,* **by Pierre-Paul Prud'hon**

flesh tones. Prud'hon found several admirers among David's pupils, notably Anne Louis Girodet (1767–1824), whose drift toward romantic themes earned him the disapproval of his master. *The Burial of Atala* (Plate 9), for example, is smoothly classical in execution, but the subject is one taken not from classical mythology, but from a contemporary work by Chateaubriand, the full title of which is *Atala, ou les amours de deux sauvages dans le desert*—"Atala, or the Love of Two Savages in the Desert." Both the maiden about to be buried and her impassioned lover are American Indians, as interpreted by the romantic imagination of nineteenth-century France.

Some of David's other followers were simpler and more straight-forward. Pierre Narcisse Guérin (1774–1833), in his portrait of his daughter (Plate 10), has made an affectionate study of child-hood. There is a disarming charm in the posing of her head and shoulders against a clear, blue sky which sets off the blond brilliancy of her coloring. Jacques Laurent Agasse (1767–1849), on the other hand, was one of the few French classicists seriously interested in animal life. His *Portrait of M. Fazy* (Plate 11) would resemble David's portraits were it not for the fact that Monsieur Fazy is put on equal footing with his horse and his dog. Agasse's paintings of animals enjoyed such popularity in England that George IV commanded him to paint the giraffe which had been given to him by Mohammed Ali Pasha and which was installed in the royal menagerie at Windsor Park.

9. *The Burial of Atala,* **by Anne Louis Girodet**

Jean Auguste Dominique Ingres (1780–1867) was unquestionably the most brilliant of David's pupils, and perhaps the greatest
of neoclassicists.   Ingres, like his master David, went to Rome
when in his twenties and remained there for eighteen years, returning to France in 1824, shortly before David's death in Belgium.
Like David he was profoundly moved by the ancient works he
found in Rome, and like David he turned, with his youthful
imagination, to scenes from classical mythology, as in *Oedipus
and the Sphinx* or *Jupiter and Thetis.*   But the France to which he

10. *Portrait of the Artist's Daughter,* by Pierre Narcisse Guérin

returned was not David's France. Following Napoleon's collapse
a new generation of artists, led by Géricault and Delacroix, had
come to the fore, disregarding classical discipline in favor of vital
emotions expressed in animated brushwork, rhythmic design, and
rich, glowing color.

Ingres had little use for dramatically contrasted tone, and
despised vivacity of touch or line. He detested anything that
suggested spontaneity, and flickering effects of light which involved the placing of lively flecks and accents of brilliant hue

11. *Portrait of M. Fazy,* **by Jacques Laurent Agasse**

among the shadows were particularly distasteful to him. Instead he applied pigment simply to give brilliant clarity to forms already sharply outlined and shadowed. This technique, together with the quiet movement of his figures and the impersonal, enamellike smoothness of his surfaces, something he shared with David and Gérard, gave his pictures an almost unearthly quality. The *Bather of Valpinçon* (Plate 12) is a perfect example. But for the flesh tones of the bather's smooth, reposed back, it is almost a symphony in whites—a thousand different shades of white melting into one another to form the coverlet, wall draperies, the bather's headcloth. As we see in this painting, Ingres, like David, believed that the function of line was to enclose and define a clear and uncomplicated shape.

Classicist though he was in his art, Ingres hid an exceedingly passionate nature beneath the austerity of his artistic principles. His ardent and impulsive side is typified by his courtship of his wife. He proposed to her by letter, and they met for the first time at Nero's tomb. He instantly fell in love with her and continued to adore her until she died, thirty-six years later, leaving him distraught and unable to work for many months.

As neoclassicism in painting was largely inspired by the Napoleonic ideal and Napoleon's patronage, it is hardly surprising that, despite the natural spread of styles from one country to another, there were few great neoclassic painters outside of France. Napoleon's campaigns deeply disrupted life in almost every country in continental Europe, and in France as well. In the words of Arthur Bryant, author of *The Age of Elegance,*

> Wherever the warring armies had been they had left behind them a slime of ruin, privation and disease. It stretched from Moscow to Antwerp, from Lisbon to Toulouse, from Leipzig to the heights of Montmartre. . . . Behind the sacrifices and romance of war lay a dreary landscape of decay and sadness; of dead horses and shattered homes, churches converted into stables and hospitals, deserted bivouacs covered with ordure, ashes, rags and broken crockery. The sick and wounded lay on heaps of straw in village streets or dragged their mangled limbs along the highways, the filthy and reeking inns were

30

12. *Bather of Valpinçon,* **by Jean Auguste Dominique Ingres**

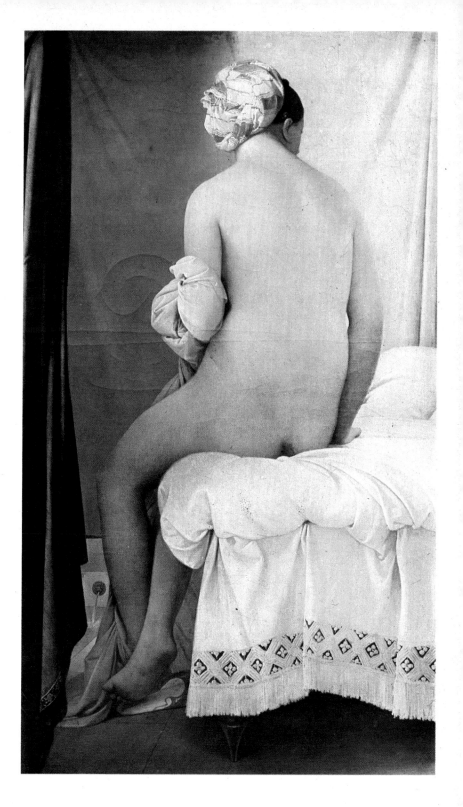

filled with troops, doors and windowsframes were torn from houses, the furniture burnt or smashed.

Such was the condition of much of continental Europe in 1814.

It is not surprising, then, that neoclassicism in the countries opposed to Napoleon—Germany, Italy, and the North countries for example—received its inspiration, not from the French imperial cult, but directly from the works of antiquity. This was originally true of the greatest of all neoclassical sculptors, the Italian Canova. Antonio Canova (1757–1822) was born in Passagno, near Venice, and came to Rome when he was twenty-two. Here he met the Scottish archaeologist Gavin Hamilton, who opened his eyes to Roman antiquities, and from then on his works, frequently figures from classical mythology, such as his *Venus* (Plate 13) were based upon Roman models. In some respects his classicism was purer and more inflexible than David's. David—and also Ingres—were, as we have seen, immediately engaged by the personality of the sitter, and this took some precedence over classical laws, but when Canova executed a portrait, he preferred to ignore the accidents of his subject, the characteristic way he held his head or sat upon a chair, and he transformed his sitters into classical deities or rulers.

Canova scored his initial success when he was commissioned to execute the tomb of Pope Clement XIV. Later he attracted the attention of Napoleon and went to Paris to make the preliminary studies for a colossal statue of the Emperor. The result was a huge bronze nude figure resembling Napoleon only slightly in the profile, and, but for details of hair and drapery, almost indistinguishable from the many representations of their rulers which the Romans had scattered about their empire: a symmetrically perfect male nude, leaning slightly on one foot, the opposite arm upraised, a form of grace and magnificence, god and emperor in one. Every detail is meticulously carved, and the applied ornament adds a touch of brilliance. Canova's surfaces were always finely chiseled and buffed to a rarefied smoothness, and this quality of finish became the goal of countless lesser sculptors during the century.

13. *Venus,* **by Antonio Canova**

The revival of classical forms was as important in the field of architecture as in those of painting and sculpture. Neoclassical architects did not merely employ classical elements—the Greek or Roman column, generally in the Doric or Ionic order, supporting the pediment with its triangular entablature—in original ways to decorate the facades of their buildings, as the architects of the Renaissance had done, but they attempted to return to the true proportions of the great buildings of Greece and Rome, thus following principles yet more strict than those governing painting and sculpture, and in some instances they strove to reproduce these buildings line for line. In his effort to turn Paris into a latter-day Rome, Napoleon initiated the construction of the Arc de Triomphe (Plate 14), a colossal imitation of the triumphal arches that the Roman emperors had constructed to memorialize their conquests, was designed by Jean François Chalgrin (1739–1811) to commemorate victories no less spectacular. It crowned

14. The Arc de Triomphe, Paris, designed by Jean François Chalgrin

15. Casina Valadier, Rome, designed by Giuseppe Valadier

16. The Glyptothek, Munich, designed by Leo von Klenze

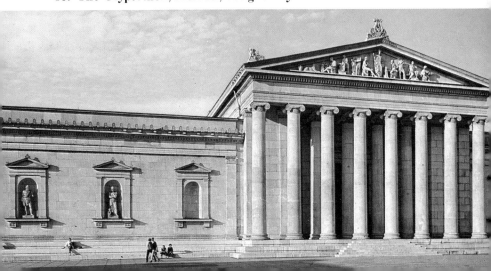

the Champs Élysées, at that time a broad and pleasant country highway leading to the Palace of the Louvre and the heart of Paris. Napoleon was responsible, too, for the first steps toward the total replanning of Paris, with its wide avenues and impressive views. Unfortunately the ordered vistas that were hewn out of the maze of streets of eighteenth-century Paris had their origin to some extent in the gruesome expedient of preventing civil insurrection—they made it easier to see a crowd from a distance and the broad avenues were more suited for the firing of cannons.

Neoclassical architecture was not reserved for France alone. Overlooking the Piazza del Popolo, as well as the rest of Rome, is the jewellike Casina Valadier (Plate 15), a small pavilion with an elegant circular colonnade, designed by Napoleon's own architect, Giuseppe Valadier (1762–1839) for his son, the King of Rome.

German archaeologists and architects had developed a passion for Roman and, particularly, Greek ideas, and they adapted their principles to public buildings wherever possible. The Glyptothek in Munich (Plate 16), designed by Leo von Klenze (1784–1864), is a handsome example. The impressions that Klenze absorbed on his travels to Greece are reflected in its facade, although the windowless walls with statuary niches that flank the colonnaded center section are largely his own invention. The interior belies the austerity of the exterior; the ceiling of the gallery is composed of small domes which give a surprisingly light and graceful effect.

A *Glyptothek* is a museum devoted to the exhibition of sculpture. It was Napoleon who started the vogue for giving art to the people by means of the creation of museums, and he filled the Palace of the Louvre with great works he had seized in foreign capitals, thus making them available to the French people. These were to provide a source of inspiration for future generations of artists and to extend the enjoyment of art beyond the confines of the aristocracy. As a result of a new civic spirit, museums sprang up all over Europe.

England enjoyed a period of great social stability in the early nineteenth century, of cultural enrichment and development at 36 home and of expansion abroad. The Napoleonic Wars did not have the disastrous effect on England that they had on the Continent, and the affluent English aristocracy and growing class of industrialists wished to assert their position with a display of wealth in the form of splendid residences. Moreover, the British had become aware of town planning, and George IV was particularly anxious to beautify his capital. He was fortunate in having John Nash (1752–1835), one of the most brilliant architects of the period, to assist him. Nash submitted several tremendously ambitious schemes, Regent's Park and the plan for Regent's Street among them. Unquestionably his greatest achievement was the Regent's Park terraces, the blocks of houses designed to face the park itself. Cumberland Terrace (Plate 17) is a perfect example of Nash's genius for applying classical forms to urban dwellings and of his complete originality. The central section, when viewed from the front, appears to be simply a pedimented temple facade, but in fact Nash has detached the pediment from the columned order and placed it on a recessed attic story.

Most of Nash's schemes were never fully realized, but they were all conceived with deliberate concern for what we would call city planning. Regent's Park was to be a garden suburb for the aristocracy, a place of greenery and clean air. "The attraction of open space, free air and the scenery of Nature with the means and invitation of exercise on horseback or foot and in carriages shall be preserved or created in Mary-le-bone Park as allurements and motives for the wealthy part of the public to establish themselves there." Earlier, in 1797, Fordyce, a famous architect and town planner, had evolved plans which had influenced Nash and many other architects. Most squares had included in their environs quarters for the working classes and for markets. Fordyce felt that:

> in the choice of situations for markets the saving of time of the servants attending them should be considered, with which view those for Butchers' Meat, Poultry, Game, Fish and Vegetables with Fruit of every kind, foreign and domestic, should be in one quarter, with no great intervening distances; and more space should be allotted to houses for courtyards and stables, than in the heart of the Town can be had, allowing more room

17. Cumberland Terrace, Regent's Park, London, designed by John Nash

19. The Treasury Building, Washington, D.C., designed by Robert Mills

for washing, for poultry and for coals which are known to be much dearer in winter than in summer, or for any other articles that can with advantage be kept in store. Fordyce also felt that the arrangement of the sewers was a matter requiring "more consideration than may at first be supposed."

Neoclassical architecture enjoyed a special flowering in America, where the new republic, the spirit of which had done much to inspire the French Revolution, also claimed kinship with ancient republican Rome. Thomas Jefferson (1743–1826), whose varied interests more than earned him the right to be called a true Renaissance man, was a dominant force. He is remembered for the design of his own home, Monticello, and for that of the University of Virginia at Charlottesville (Plate 18), to which, after he served as President, he devoted the last nine years of his life. The college buildings, in the form of alternating Ionic and Corinthian pavilions, face each other across the stepped lawns. Behind their porticos, colonnaded and roofed entrances of white wood imposed against a facade of local red brick, they have two floors, the lower devoted to classrooms and the upper to living accomodations for the professors. They are linked by a single story Doric gallery of smaller scale that forms the open corridor for the students' rooms behind. The upper end of this "forum" is dominated by the domed library, and the whole complex, its vivid white columns standing out against the red brick and green lawns of Virginia, is a rich and vivid version of the more stark adaptation of classical forms seen elsewhere.

Washington, D.C., the new capital, was of course meant to represent the very best of neoclassical planning, and might well have become a perfect representation of its ideals. But when, in 1790, it was laid out by Pierre Charles L'Enfant (1754–1825), it took the form of a hunting park rather than a metropolis. L'Enfant's architectural vision was not of walled-in streets and squares; it was governed instead by the isolated block-like structures that were to stand around the radiating circles of avenues like sentinels. The major monuments of the 1830's still stand in Washington, most of them designed by Robert Mills (1781–1855) at the peak of his career. His Treasury Building (Plate 39) is an elegant exercise in the Ionic order, set against a background of Doric pilasters, columns standing flat against the facade, that frame the three tiers of windows.

The first Capitol, for the design of which there had been a competition, was conceived in 1792 by William Thornton (1759–1828) and completed by Charles Bulfinch (1763–1844) in 1830. The central section is all that remains of the original simple and elegant plan. The additions of Thomas Walter (1804–1887) in the mid-nineteenth century, the flanking wings and cast-iron dome, introduced a completely different scale and obscured the original intention. Still and all, the city itself, with its great avenues and splendid views, stands as a monument to the neoclassical spirit.

It must not be thought that any one movement in art dies when another is born. On the contrary, they always overlap, and frequently influence each other. The seeds of romanticism, the movement which combatted and eventually overthrew neoclassicism, are to be found in the eighteenth century, and romanticism had had its flow and ebb before the death of the greatest of the neoclassicists, Ingres. Ingres lived throughout the better part of the century, and his style, the formal concepts he had in-

18. The University of Virginia, Charlottesville, designed by Thomas Jefferson

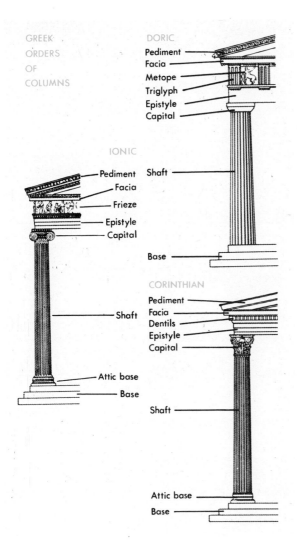

GREEK
ORDERS
OF
COLUMNS

DORIC
Pediment
Facia
Metope
Triglyph
Epistyle
Capital

Shaft

Base

IONIC
Pediment
Facia
Frieze
Epistyle
Capital

Shaft

Attic base
Base

CORINTHIAN
Pediment
Facia
Dentils
Epistyle
Capital

Shaft

Attic base
Base

herited from David, he retained to the end. His painting changed so little throughout his lifetime that he was able to use the bather of Valpinçon, slightly transposed, as the central figure of another work fifty-five years later, when the impressionist movement was already under way.

41

Romanticism

WHAT IS MEANT by "the romantic movement"? Many books have been written in an attempt to explain all phases of romanticism, but the term remains a catchall phrase denoting a group of movements having one thing in common—freedom from constraint. It meant freedom from the constraint of classical forms and the smooth tightness of neoclassical technique, in literature as well as art. It meant freedom to feel and voice, and even paint, strong emotions. It meant freedom to leave the confines of society and return to nature, freedom to quit the confines of Europe and wander in distant lands, freedom to escape into any period of the past, to explore the mysteries of alien cultures, and even the mysteries of the interior mind.

The classicists created, as we have seen, the cult of the hero. For them he represented an image of stern, implacable force, but for the romantics he was a being possessed. Byron was their ideal, and with the cult of the romantic hero came the cult of genius, and an almost morbid concern with personality, sometimes to the point of madness. The dominant emotion was one of nervous melancholy. These preoccupations led frequently to a gloomy pondering on death, and suicide became the ultimate romantic gesture of despair.

But if the prevailing mood was one of sadness, when joy came it flooded and intoxicated the romantic spirit and the artist was possessed by a feeling of lyrical ecstasy, which resulted, for instance, in the pastoral paintings of Samuel Palmer (Plate 20). William Blake, both poet and painter, who had a profound influence on Palmer, once described energy as "eternal delight." In positive terms romanticism spurred on ardent nationalists and revolutionaries. Artists, poets, and composers desired to feel at one with the irresistible force of Nature, which they saw as something infinitely good and beautiful and, at the same time, horribly awesome and threatening. Allied to this was an obsession with the effects of weather and atmosphere, with light and

20. *In a Shoreham Garden,* **by Samuel Palmer**

color. Turner lashed himself to the main mast of a ship to record the fury of a tempest, and Wordsworth wandered about the countryside reflecting on the mysterious shadows cast by clouds scudding above the lakes and mountainsides, while John Ruskin, the great critic, wrote his finest passages of descriptive prose to capture the wild beauty of an Alpine storm or the fireflies in the sunset outside the gates of Siena.

Probably the first of the true romantics was Francisco José de Goya y Lucientes, born in the Spanish province of Aragon in 1746. Goya's early career and his rise to the position of court painter to Charles IV were simple and unexceptional. The son of a master gilder, he studied first in Spain and then in Italy, win-

43

ning second place in a competition held by the Parma Academy in 1771. Later that year he returned to Spain, where he executed several frescoes and a large number of "cartoons," or designs for tapestries, and enjoyed increasing recognition. In 1780 he was elected to the Academy and quickly found work as a portrait painter. In 1785 he was appointed Deputy Director of Painting at the Academy; the following year he was nominated Painter to the King; and in 1789, on the accession of Charles IV, he was appointed *Pintor de Cámara*. Commissions also came from other sources, notably from the Duke of Osuna, for whom he did portraits and a series of decorative panels. By the age of forty Goya was established, with a good income which he appears to have spent lavishly. He lived exuberantly, and is even said to have fought in the bullring.

Goya's style during this time was facile, brilliant, and in the best tradition of eighteenth-century portraiture and decoration. A good example of his earlier works is his graceful tapestry cartoon, *The Sunshade* (Plate 21), executed for the Palace of El Pardo. It was at this period, too, that he painted a portrait of himself (Plate 22). Were it not for something strange in the look of the artist's eyes, we would have no hint of what was to come.

In the year 1792 Goya's career was violently halted by an illness which temporarily paralyzed his hands and left him permanently deaf. It must have seemed, for almost two years, that he had come to the end of his career. But his constitution was enormously strong. He began painting again late in 1793, and it is from that moment that his major achievements can be dated. His deafness was a terrible tragedy for a man who reveled in considerable social success, and from now on the sinister undertones which had appeared fleetingly in his earlier pictures began to dominate his imagination. But there was in Goya's later paintings and drawings a macabre element that sprang from something more than the loneliness which his deafness had inflicted upon him. It sprang from the visions of a mind that saw evil as a supernatural force.

When he began the series of pictures which first fully disclosed his personal vision, he wrote to his friend, the diplomat Bernardo

21. *The Sunshade,* **tapestry cartoon, by Francisco José de Goya y Lucientes**

de Yriarte, "to engage my imagination which had been almost deadened by constant brooding over my sufferings ... I have ventured upon a few cabinet pictures. In these paintings I have been able to make observations which ordinarily there is not the opportunity to make in commissioned works, and in which fantasy and invention are given full rein." The inner vision of the artist, freed from the necessity of pleasing a patron—this is the very essence of what was to become the romantic movement. "Romantic" artists of a later date strove to express the most intense mo-

22. *Self-Portrait,* **by Francisco José de Goya y Lucientes**

ments of joy and suffering. Goya was supreme in expressing the latter.

It was at this time that he painted the courtyard of a madhouse, in which "two naked madmen are struggling with the warder, who is striking them. . . . I saw such an incident in Saragossa." Between 1795 and 1798 he painted six scenes of witchcraft for the Countess-Duchess of Osuna. For the rest of his life Goya intermittently painted pictures of cannibalism and violence, some-

times suggested by the events of the Peninsular Wars, Napoleonic

Wars in Spain, at other times drawn from plays, historical anec-
dotes, or his own imagination. In many of these small pictures
the delicacy of handling, typical of his earlier work, remains.
They are often an incongruous blend of macabre subject and
elegant technique. Thin veils of paint create a soft, glowing atmosphere which caresses these frightful forms as tenderly as earlier it had wrapped about the silks and glowing faces of his cour-
tiers. Goya's monsters perform their atrocities in the tranquility
of a late-summer's evening. Such a work of profoundly disturbing
symbolism is *The Colossus,* a giant figure with fists clenched,
looms over a panic-stricken caravan. The colossus is at once
the cause and the embodiment of the travelers' terror. This
supernatural apparition is not a symbol of their fear; it is its visible
manifestation.

By no means are all of Goya's later works so forbidding, and
he was still capable of painting the smiling *Majas on a Balcony,*
but his huge and formal *Family of Charles IV* (Plate 23) betrays
Goya's harshness once again in his view of the king and queen and
their entourage. Never has a royal family been less flatteringly
portrayed. Both the king and his queen are endowed with a mind-
less ugliness, and Goya is kind only in his rendering of the children.
This portrait was painted in 1800, shortly after the publication of
Los Caprichos.

Los Caprichos, "The Caprices," was an album of eighty etchings,
a peculiar blend of social and political satire and horrifying fantasy. In his advertisement in the *Diario de Madrid,* published in
1799, Goya announced that the purpose of these capricious pictures was to ridicule "the multitude of follies and blunders common in every civil society." Of the first forty-two plates, the
majority show the life of his earlier tapestry cartoons stripped of
its gaiety. These are the same *majos* and *majas* (loose men and
women of the street) who laughed and picnicked lightheartedly
in the verdant landscapes he had designed to hang on the walls
of El Pardo. But now the earth is barren, the sky obscured.
Laughter freezes into inhuman grimaces. Each soul is locked into
a solitary confinement. The instrument of human communica-
tion, the face, is a mask of deceit. Only once in the eighty plates 47

23. *Family of Charles IV,* by Francisco José de Goya y Lucientes

of *Caprichos* does the gaze of two pairs of eyes meet. In Plate 6 a man and a woman stare intently, blankly, at each other through the slits of masks. The title is *Nobody Knows Anybody,* and Goya comments, "The world is a masquerade; face, dress, voice, everything is feigned."

In Plate 43 of *Los Caprichos* (Plate 24) Goya announces the theme of the subsequent plates with an image of the artist asleep, surrounded by bats and other monstrous symbols of ignorance and madness. This is the famous *Sleep of Reason Which Produces Monsters.* Goya's additional comment was, "Imagination, deserted by reason, begets impossible monsters. United with reason, she is the mother of all arts, and the source of their wonders." Yet Goya was no rationalist merely satirizing human folly. The monsters he created are the incarnation of his own unbridled imagination. It is in his comprehension of the evil and depravity

24. *Los Caprichos,* **(No. 43), by Francisco José de Goya y Lucientes**

25. *The Witches Sabbath* (detail), by Francisco José de Goya y Lucientes

possible in the human imagination, his own no less than that of other men, that the secret of *Los Caprichos* lies.

What is perhaps most amazing about Goya is the tolerance with which he was treated. Despite his bitter satires on the immorality and corruption of Spanish society and the Church in *Los Caprichos,* he was shortly afterward appointed Principal Painter to the King. Moreover, being politically a liberal, he had sided with the new French republic waging war on Charles IV, and in 1808, when Spain was invaded by Napoleon and Ferdinand VII was replaced by Joseph Bonaparte, Goya defected to the French side; nevertheless, when Ferdinand was restored to power after Napoleon's defeat, one of his first acts was to forgive Goya's defection and reinstate him. As for *Los Caprichos,* only twenty-seven sets of the first edition were sold, and shortly thereafter Goya offered the plates and 240 unsold sets to the king in exchange for a pension for his son Javier.

Meanwhile, with increasing age, Goya's inner life became more intense. In 1819 he bought a country house outside Madrid, which he proceeded to decorate with sinister fantasies called the *Pinturas Negras,* or Black Pictures. Now the nightmare effect is intensified by a dense black modeling that has replaced the sparkling palette of his youth. It is accompanied by a bold experimental handling, which sometimes even involved the use of sponges to smudge the paint and give his surfaces breadth and freedom. This also had the effect of brutalizing the forms. If we look, for example, at *The Witches Sabbath* (Plate 25), we can see what a terrifying turn the mind which produced the portrait of young Don Manuel Osorio has taken. Indeed, witchcraft had occupied Goya's thoughts for many years. At the witches' Sabbath the novice witches are brought by their mistresses to the Meadow of the Great Goat and presented to the devil, who orders them to make merry. But the degradation that Goya portrays is entirely human.

Both *The Pilgrimage to the Miraculous Fountain of S. Isidoro* (Plate 26) and *The Fantastic Vision* (Plate 27) are among the Black Pictures. In the former the nutcracker-jawed and bloated figures are terrifying, but in the latter, were it not for the always sinister touch—the soldier on the right taking aim— the scene would be almost lyrically beautiful. In these paintings it is hard to say precisely what is happening. As in a bad dream half remembered, the dark meaning is only suggested, rarely told. In the extraordinarily decorated villa from which the Black Pictures came, the aging artist took his meals confronted by the image of a demented *Saturn Devouring His Son.*

When he was seventy-eight, Goya came under suspicion from the authorities for his liberal political views and went into voluntary exile in France. He died four years later, in 1828.

At the turn of the nineteenth century Goya was outside the mainstream of art. His work was not part of a movement; he was simply a brilliant eighteenth-century portraitist strangely moved by an inner vision he expressed. But soon enough the great brooding figure of Byron would wander the face of Europe, an eloquent exile, guilty of nameless crimes. Literature was moving toward the lyric, the passionate, the personal, although austere neoclassicism still reigned in the visual arts, and continued to do so until after the fall of Napoleon.

Early in the century a group of young painters in France, led by Jean Louis André Théodore Géricault (1791–1824) and Eugène Delacroix (1798–1863), sought to free themselves from the inflexible order established by the neoclassicists, with their fixed laws of composition and clearly defined ideal forms.

Géricault, the older of the two, was the first deliberately to break away. He studied the classicists and at the age of twenty-four, following an unhappy love affair, went to Rome, where he visited Ingres in his studio, but he was most deeply impressed by the works of Michelangelo, in front of which, he later recalled, he trembled with emotion. Meanwhile, his enthusiasm for David and Napoleon led him to the paintings of Gros, who influenced him deeply. He began to feel the power and flexibility of the brush, and developed, as a result, a highly free and original technique, spirited and dramatic, in which the quality of the individual strokes, thick or thin, soft or sharp, could convey a great range of emotions.

His earliest paintings, inspired by Napoleon's greatest triumphs, 53

26. *The Pilgrimage to the Miraculous Fountain of S. Isidoro,* by Francisco José de Goya y Lucientes
27. *The Fantastic Vision,* by Francisco José de Goya y Lucientes

depicted battle scenes—wounded cavalry men and and command-
ers upon their chargers. His depiction of *An Officer of the Chausseurs Charging* (Plate 28) was painted before his trip to Rome, and
displays how, in even his earliest works, he was capable of the most
vigorous design. The horse's rippling mane, the thick smoke,
the distant flashes of light and shadow sum up the very essence
of the romantic sense of the dramatic. It is suprising, therefore,
that Gericault's master was none other than the passive classicist
Guérin.

As he matured, Géricault turned to subjects that were essen-

28. *An Officer of the Chausseurs Charging,* **by Jean Louis
André Théodore Géricault**

tially unglamorous, and expressed the deeper levels of human desolation. During this period of his life he worked long hours by candlelight in the Paris morgue, depicting executed prisoners (Plate 29), suicides, and victims of murder. He went so far as to keep a severed head wrapped in a napkin on his kitchen table so that he could observe the effects of decomposition. Always a nervous and sensitive young man, he was almost unhinged by such concentration. He retained his sanity, however, possibly through the daily discipline of life classes in Guérin's studio.

From his earliest years Géricault had been fascinated by horses.

29. *A Study of Heads of Executed Prisoners,* by Jean Louis André Théodore Géricault

30. *The Horse Stopped by Slaves,* by Jean Louis André
Théodore Géricault

He was entranced, as Goethe had been, by the horseracing that took place in the Corso in Rome. During his stay there he produced a series of vivid sketches for a finished work that was to be entitled *The Race of the Riderless Horse*. As we can see from one of these studies, *The Horse Stopped by Slaves* (Plate 30), the finished picture was to be classical in setting, although it was to have a spirited romantic flavor.

Guérin described Géricault as "three or four artists rolled into one." It is ironic that he was killed in a riding accident at the age of thirty-two. His death left Eugène Delacroix, his close friend for many years, the undisputed leader of the romantic movement in French painting.

Though officially the son of a minister under the Directory, that short-lived post-Revolutionary French government, Delacroix was rumored to have been in fact the son of Talleyrand, the greatest political manipulator of his day and the most powerful man in early nineteenth-century France, with the exception of Napoleon himself. In any case, Delacroix attracted the attention of the leaders of society. He was handsome in a tigerlike way, as the poet Baudelaire remarked; he was something of a Beau Brummell in matters of dress; he was exceptionally well-read, especially in English literature; and his sophisticated wit made him the welcome guest of the ladies of Paris society. Though reserved in manner he enjoyed parties and the company of women, yet was capable of going off by himself for long periods in order to concentrate upon his painting.

Most of Delacroix's works portray scenes and events remote from his own time, and often remote from reality, scenes of historical, mythological, biblical, or literary inspiration. And in his depiction of these subjects he concentrated on the dramatic, critical moments of battles, of hunts, or of fights between animals. This is the "pure" romanticism of stormy, thrilling subject matter, far from everyday existence.

In Delacroix's paintings the clear outline of the classicists is completely lost. As the artist himself wrote, "When the tones are right, the lines draw themselves." But he did not arrive at such a happy conclusion without a struggle. In this he was influ- 59 enced most deeply by the vivid color and swift fresh strokes of Rubens, and furthermore when his contemporary, Constable, exhibited *The Hay Wain* at the Salon, Delacroix was so overwhelmed by its sparkling outdoor light that he withdrew his own *Massacre at Chios* so that he could repaint the background. Above all, like Gericault, he was able to capture the most violent action in a brushstroke.

31. *Liberty Guiding the People,* **by Eugene Delacroix.**

When Delacroix dealt with a current event, he lifted it beyond the realm of reality. His *Liberty Guiding the People* (Plate 31) commemorates the revolutionary upheavals of Paris in 1830. Here a very realistic painting of the Paris masses in revolt is dominated by the symbolic, totally imaginary figure of Liberty, who heroically emerges from the gun smoke to lead her followers while mightily grasping the tricolor in one of the most gallant gestures

in all the history of painting. This is a rare example of a picture in which a symbolic figure has been successfully incorporated with realistic action.

Delacroix had always reveled in the exotic, and the six months that he spent in Morocco in 1832 were to remain an inspiration to him for the rest of his life. On the same voyage that took him to Morocco he also visited Spain, where he saw the works of Velasquez and Goya. From Goya he learned anew how a simplified

32. *Women of Algiers*, by **Eugène Delacroix**

although shadowy silhouette could instantly and dramatically convey action to the beholder.

His Spanish experiences reinforced in his memory the essence of the North African scene, and Delacroix painted a number of pictures of Arabs fighting or hunting, and an epic series of lions and tigers. On his return from Spain he commenced the *Women of Algiers* (Plate 32), for which he made a vast number of preparatory drawings, detailing the decor and objects he had actually seen on a visit to a Moroccan harem and trying to recapture a mood of seductive indolence. Over twenty years after his trip to North Africa he executed a series of paintings of lion hunts which in a way crowned his career. *The Lion Hunt* (Plate 33) in the Museum of Fine Arts in Boston conveys his love for exotic Moorish trappings, and also his great interest in animals, which he studied both alive in the zoo and dead in the natural history museum. He was also influenced by the animal hunts of Rubens, which this painting resembles in that its design, like those of Rubens, is broken up into units (horsemen to the left and right, and the triangular group of lion and hunter at the bottom) that impress us not only as elements in a drama, but also as segments of a pictorial order. And, with his strange perspective in which the ground shelves up at an angle, it is almost a flat design rather like an Oriental tapestry. As we shall see, this kind of treatment had an extraordinary effect upon his admirers in the younger generation of painters.

The only sculptor of the period even occasionally able to approach Delacroix's emotional force was François Rude (1784–1855). His masterpiece, *La Marseillaise* (Plate 34), a huge relief applied to the Arc de Triomphe, is in some ways the sculptured counterpart of *Liberty Guiding the People*. It portrays the volunteers leaving to fight in the Revolutionary army of 1792. But although the spirit is romantic, the figures themselves are executed along the lines of the hardened heroic forms of classicism. Rude's student, Jean Baptiste Carpeaux (1827–1875), succeeded, by allowing the surface irregularities of his original modeling to remain visible, in achieving a technique similar to the free brushwork of the French romantic painters. In his *A Boy With a Shell Against* 63

33. *The Lion Hunt,* **by Eugène Delacroix**

35. *A Boy With a Shell Against His Ear,* **by Jean Baptiste Carpeaux**

34. *La Marseillaise,* **by François Rude**

His Ear (Plate 35), we can see that, like the painters of the romantic movement, he was able to capture a fleeting emotion or gesture. Antoine Louis Barye (1796–1875), originally trained as a painter under Gros, was perhaps most influenced by Géricault and Delacroix. Like them, he was fascinated by wild animals (Plate 36), although he could never quite invest his lions and horses with the terrible energy one sees in the works of these two masters.

But to understand the romantic movement, and the romantic painters and sculptors of Paris, it is important above all to understand that never before had art and literature been so truly allied — never had artists and writers been so close in their personal friendships or in their goals. In the eighteenth century in France artists and writers had not even been on the same social footing, for until artists were liberated by the Revolution they had, with few exceptions, been the servants of the state or a patron, generally regarded as lacking in taste, education, and manners. It was taken for granted that the best would be churlish, while, as Diderot remarked, "if you happen to meet a sculptor who is polite, gentle, well-mannered and modest, you can say he is, and always will be, *second-rate.*"

But under the Empire those who had come into wealth began to welcome artists liberally; successful artists themselves entertained intellectuals and aristocrats, and soon began to borrow appearances from them, acquiring the look of English sporting dandies. But below this level swarmed a host of lesser, poverty-stricken artists, struggling for recognition, and on their behalf the greatest writers and poets were to speak out during the first thirty or forty years of the century.

It was under the influence of Victor Hugo, the literary giant of the age, that the rapport between artist and writer really began. This was partly the result of a change in location. During the eighteenth century, while the world of books and students had crowded the Latin Quarter on the left bank of the Seine in Paris, artists had been concentrated in Montmartre, on the right bank, and around the Louvre. But from the turn of the century onward there was a steady drift of artists to the left bank, David, Ingres, and Delacroix all taking part. In 1824 Hugo moved to a house on 67

36. *Jaguar Devouring a Crocodile,* by Antoine Louis Barye

the left bank next to the Jardin du Luxembourg, and his home was to become the center of exchange for romantic ideas. At that time, however, the area was rather squalid, and the Hugos would escape back over the Seine to civilized society once a week—to the home of Charles Nodier. Nodier, a librarian at the Arsenal, an important Parisian library, had started the practice of opening his house to his friends on Sunday mornings and evenings. These delightfully informal salons were the meeting ground for all kinds of artists, writers, and critics, among them the poets Émile Deschamps, Alfred de Vigny, Lamartine, on occasions, and later the man of letters, Théophile Gautier, the novelists Honoré de Balzac and Alexandre Dumas, and Delacroix. Unlike the great salons of the eighteenth century, there was little ceremony, and no brilliant *salonnière* presiding over her guests. They drank lemonade (gooseberry wine on festive occasions), danced, and sat on the floor when there were too few chairs, while the greatest artists remained aloof and were lionized.

In 1827 Hugo moved to a larger residence near several of the young and brilliant artists of the times, in the Rue Notre-Dame-des-Champs. The publication of his preface to *Cromwell,* a manifesto of the new rules of literature and the fine arts, now gave him the authority and confidence to set up a salon of his own. Artists and writers alike could join in his denunciation of the classicists and his plea for more vitality and local color in the arts.

"We demand a verse which is free, honest, and straightforward, that dares in all things to avoid prudery and affectation; . . . that is both realistic and poetic, at once beautifully wrought and genuinely inspired; that has depth yet spontaneity, breadth yet truth."

Hugo's circle, though the reputations of many of its members fell into decline or were neglected, was in general more talented, more experienced than Nodier's. Hugo was looked upon as the great romantic leader—a twin pillar with Delacroix. In fact his *Orientales* (colorful, dramatic poems of the East) reminds one strongly of Delacroix's paintings of North Africa. He continued to open his house to an increasing number of young and promising artists, while the older and busier circle dwindled. One of the most colorful of these youthful supporters was Théophile Gautier, who was wavering in his choice of a career between literature and art. His writings describe the enthusiasm of artists not necessarily known to Hugo, for the romantic revolution:

Much reading was done in the studios. The *rapins* (young pupils) were fond of literature, and their specialized training, which had put them in close touch with nature, made them readily appreciative of the imagery and colour in the new poetry . . . .

What marvellous days! Walter Scott was then in full flower of his success; we were being initiated into the mysteries of Goethe's *Faust,* a work that, to use Mme. de Staël's expression, contained everything, and a little more than everything. We were discovering Shakespeare in the rather clumsy translation of Letourneur, and the poems of Lord Byron, *The Corsair, Lara, The Giaour, Manfred, Beppo, Don Juan,* were reaching us from the East, not yet becoming commonplace. How youthful, fresh, intoxicating, bizarre in colour, and highly flavoured all this was! It turned our heads; we seemed to be entering unknown worlds. At every page we came upon subjects for compositions which we hastened to draw, or dash down furtively—for such motifs would not have been to the master's taste and, had they been discovered, would have earned us a sharp rap over the head with the stick.

These young artists carried their resolution into the world of fashion, partly to express their newfound feelings, partly to shock the conservative members of the public. Eugène Deveria, in veneration of the sixteenth century, introduced a tailcoat with velvet facings and a waistcoat more like a doublet. He also waxed a pair of moustaches and wore a long pointed beard that jutted out at an angle. Hugo described the motley crowd who turned up for the first night of his controversial play *Hernani* as "wild whimsical characters, bearded, longhaired, dressed in every fashion except the reigning one, in pea-jackets, in Spanish cloaks, in waistcoats à la Robespierre, in Henry III bonnets, carrying on their heads and backs articles of costume from every century and clime, and this in the middle of Paris and in broad daylight!" But of them all Gautier was the most resplendent, with hair flowing over his shoulders and his famous waistcoat of scarlet satin. Another—Nanteuil—wore a long blue coat buttoned up to the chin, soutane-style, with his fair hair parted to one side and cut like that of a medieval student.

When Henri Murger wrote his *Scènes de la vie de Bohème* ("Scenes from Bohemian Life"), on which Puccini's opera *La Bohème* was later based, the impoverished young artists and writers of the Left Bank were endowed with a name . . . one that suggested the romantic movement to everyone in the Western world—Bohemians.

In Germany, much of romanticism was expressed by landscape painting. The same was true, as we shall see, in England. The German landscapes are often unreal in the sense that they are ideally beautiful, like the crystalline Alps in *A View of Chamonix and Mont Blanc* (Plate 37) by Julius Schnorr von Carolsfeld (1795–1872). Some are tremendously moving, like the works of Casper

David Friedrich (1774–1840). Friedrich filled his scenes with overwhelming melancholy. He was born on the Baltic coast, and these lonely northern foreshores, as well as the bare crags of the Harz Mountains, which he visited later, provided him with symbols of immensity. The subject of his painting *The Wreck of the "Hope"*

37. *A View of Chamonix and Mont Blanc,* **by Julius Schnorr von Carolsfeld**

(Plate 38) came from Captain Perry's eyewitness description of the actual scene, which the artist had read. It was the first time that a painter had attempted to depict an Arctic wreck, but in his childhood Friedrich had seen piled-up, splintered ice on the Baltic coast, and he drew on these impressions to portray an infinite, 71

38. *The Wreck of the "Hope,"* **by Casper David Friedrich**

hostile waste. Friedrich's paintings sometimes capture, in a perfect manner, the often weird spirit of German romanticism.

On July 10, 1809, a group of young painters founded the *Lukas-
bund* in Vienna—a revival of the medieval painters' guild of St.
Luke. They revolted against the academic ideas of their teachers
and attempted to revive the spirit of German sixteenth-century

paintings. As we have seen, the nineteenth century was one in which artists frequently sought inspiration from the styles of the past. The *Lukas-bund* later moved to Rome, where the painters established themselves in the disused monastery of St. Isidoro and lived a communal life as "painter-monks." Very soon they were joined by German artists, like Schnorr von Carolsfeld. One of their most important commissions was the decoration of the Casino Massimo for the Marchese Carlo Massimo. This enabled Joseph Anton Koch (1768–1839), who had become distinguished for his Alpine landscapes, to reveal another facet of his talent. He devised a vast design depicting Dante's *Divine Comedy,* in which his portrayal of the torments of the damned in the *Inferno* (Plate 39) was a deeply felt attempt to revive the terrors of a medieval hell.

Koch's tortured figures resemble in some ways those of William Blake (1757–1827), the first English romantic and one of the most totally original geniuses in the history of art. Blake was, like his contemporary Goya, a forerunner of the romantic movement and a lone experimenter in artistic expression. He was also one of the few artists ever to be a first-rate poet.

Blake was born in London, the son of a hosier. He went to drawing school at the age of ten, but was apprenticed at fifteen to a copper engraver. For seven years, he learned the trade which kept him, often to his sorrow, for much of his life. Working as a journeyman, he engraved designs for other inferior artists for over fifty publications.

In his greatest works, the two sides of Blake's genius are fused. These are his illuminated books, etched on copper by his own process, in which the text, written by hand, and the illustrations are complementary, and hard to separate. These range from the *Songs of Innocence* (1789) to the difficult symbolic poems, *Milton* (1804–1808) and *Jerusalem* (1804–1820). During his lifetime, these works remained almost unknown.

Blake's art was almost entirely illustrative, and it is just as well that his works were generally on a small scale, carried out mostly in pen and watercolor, for when they are enlarged, they sometimes reveal a weakness in structure. However, whether embellishing 73

his own writings or those of others, his pictures are not illustrations in the strict sense. Like Goya's *Caprichos,* they are the result of an inner vision expressed in pictorial form; they are also deeply imaginative, and they somehow transcend the actual meaning of what they illustrate. Blake believed that the only important knowledge was that which existed before birth, and which at birth was obscured by the flesh.

Above all, Blake was profoundly religious. He believed that "the man who never in his mind and thoughts travel'd to Heaven is no Artist." He felt that rationalism and the Newtonian reduction of the universe to mechanical order, by seeking for a material explanation of the world, led to spiritual death and reduced man to an automaton. The artist's visionary power was ignored, reducing him to a craftsman mechanically copying the appearances of things seen with his physical eye. This single view to Blake was no better than sleep: "What! it will be questioned. When the sun rises do you not see a round disc of fire somewhat like a guinea? O no! No! I see an innumerable company of the heavenly host crying 'Holy Holy Holy is the Lord God Almighty.'"

His claim that he possessed visionary powers earned him the reputation of madness. At the request of his friends, he drew the portraits of the long-dead William Wallace and Edward I as if from living sitters. He claimed that the prophets Isaiah and Ezekiel had dined with him, that he was under the direction of "messengers from Heaven Daily and Nightly," and that he wrote his poem *Milton* "from immediate dictation . . . without Premeditation and even against my Will."

At his memorable dinner with the prophets Blake claimed to have asked Isaiah how he dared to assert so roundly that God had spoken to him. Isaiah answered, "I saw no God, nor heard any, in a finite organic perception; but my senses discover'd the infinite in everything, and I was then persuaded, and remain confirm'd—that the voice of honest indignation is the voice of God."

Pity (Plate 40), which is among the most moving and haunting of Blake's inventions, is neither a caprice nor a projection of some strange and obscure vision whose meaning is known only to the artist. It is a visual translation of the beautiful metaphor spoken   75

39. *Hell* **(detail from the frescoes in the Dante room), by Joseph Anton Koch**

40. *Pity,* **by William Blake**

by Macbeth at the beginning of Act I, scene vii, in which he debates the murder of Duncan.

> And pity, like a naked new-born babe
> Striding the blast, or Heaven's cherubir
>   hors'd

41. *The House of Death,* **by William Blake**

> Upon the sightless couriers of the air,
> Shall blow the horrid deed in every eye,
> That tears shall drown the wind."

The House of Death (Plate 41), like *Pity,* is color-printed by a
system which was Blake's own invention. Also like *Pity,* it is the   77

42. *Nebuchadnezzar,* **by William Blake**

44. *Newton,* **by William Blake**

45. *The Ancient of Days*, by William Blake

illustration or visual translation of lines by a great English poet, this time Milton. Blake has taken the prophetic vision of misery and disaster consequent on the fall of man which Michael presents to Adam in the eleventh book of *Paradise Lost*. In his later years Blake found inspiration in Milton's works not only for his own poetry, but for many of his finest pictures.

Nebuchadnezzar (Plate 42) is likewise in some ways a very literal illustration, in fact so literal that it is terrifying. The fourth chapter of the Book of Daniel relates how Nebuchadnezzar had a strange dream, which the prophet Daniel interpreted as signifying "that they shall drive thee from men, and thy dwelling shall be with the beasts of the field, and they shall make thee to eat grass as oxen . . . till thou know that the Most High ruleth in the kingdom of men." Before the end of a year this prophecy was fulfilled and Nebuchadnezzar, who was King of Babylon, was driven from men and, grown mad, did eat grass as oxen, "and his body was wet with the dew of heaven, till his hairs were grown like eagles' feathers, and his nails like birds' claws." At the end of his punishment the King regained his sanity and acknowledged the power and goodness of God and was restored to his former greatness.

Satan Smiting Job with Sore Boils (Plate 43) is a powerful rendition of a scene from the Book of Job, for which Blake engraved a series of illustrations toward the end of his life. The pattern of Satan's wings repeated in the clouds over the sun creates an effect of the most sinister foreboding. Blake's sense of design is in all cases strong. The compass represented for him the rationality of the material world, and it is interesting to see it in the hand of Newton in his painting of that great scientist (Plate 44); it also appears as the focal point for his splendid composition, *The Ancient of Days* (Plate 45). Few artists, with the exception of Michelangelo, have possessed the courage or the ability to create, with the force of Blake, a figure suggesting God the Father.

Blake's work was independent of any specific movement in art, although he served to some extent as an inspiration for later romantics. Two other painters of the nineteenth century closely resembled him in both their philosophy and their work. One was

Samuel Palmer (1805–1881), who met and befriended Blake in

43. *Satan Smiting Job with Sore Boils,* **by William Blake**

1824, the year before his death. Palmer was primarily a landscapist, and like Blake, he too was a visionary artist, but the nature of his vision was fixed early in life, as he vividly recalled later when he wrote of his nanny:

> who with little education else, was ripe in that without which so much is often useless or mischievous: deeply read in her Bible and *Paradise Lost*. A Tonson's Milton which I treasure to this day, was her present. When less than four years old, as I was standing with her, watching the shadows on the wall from the branches of an elm behind which the moon had risen, she transferred and fixed the fleeting image in my memory by repeating the couplet:
>
>> Vain man, the vision of a moment made,
>> Dream of a dream and shadow of a shade.

He dwelt with remarkable single-mindedness on the image of a fruitful idyllic countryside, inspired by his reading of Vergil and sanctified by Christian belief. Nature was presented as unsullied and burgeoning; huge stalks stand ripening in the fields, and the orchard boughs bend beneath the weight of their fruit. In his painting entitled *In a Shoreham Garden* (Plate 20), Palmer's use of gouache, a medium thicker than watercolor but lighter than oil paint, gives the impression of overwhelming abundance. Every detail has been introduced as an image of nature's fecundity, and the color is more the expression of an inner sensation of golden nature than anything that might actually meet the eye.

The other artist who resembled Blake in many ways could not possibly have known him. Albert Pinkham Ryder (1847–1917) was an American born twenty years after Blake died. Ryder grew up among the sailing men of the whaling port of New Bedford, Massachusetts, and at the age of twenty he moved to New York, where he became a recluse, rarely leaving his small apartment. Like Blake he was an isolated romantic, whose style owed little to previous schools or individual painters and was a completely original response to his own inner reflections. He was haunted by his early memories of the sea, and by the imaginary landscapes of Edgar Allan Poe:

> Dim vales and shadowy floods
> And cloudy looking woods . . . .

He painted strange, symbolic pictures with simplified, distorted forms that arranged themselves into a pattern of great dark masses. He frequently painted landscapes in which small figures floated unconsciously, suggesting the inhabitants of a dream. He loved to paint moonlight, and as we can see in his *Fisherman's Cottage* (Plate 46), he captured it with a mood of eerie reality. Unfortunately this canvas shows deterioration, as Ryder's self-taught technique was to load the pigment on so thickly that the uneven surface looked like a painted clay relief. After less than a century his paints have cracked and darkened.

In England the great romantics, with the exception of Blake, were landscape painters. In the eighteenth century the vogue for "picturesque" landscapes was such that special glasses were available through which one could look at a framed view of the countryside. Edward Ferrars in Jane Austen's *Sense and Sensibility* (written in 1797) accuses Marianne of wanting "every book that tells how to admire an old twisted tree," and amateur landscapists cropped up in every family. In Austen's *Northanger Abbey* (written in 1798), Henry Tilney is careful to teach Catherine Moreland how to observe a landscape:

> The Tilneys were viewing the country with the eyes of persons accustomed to drawing, and deciding on its capability of being formed into pictures, with all the eagerness of real taste. Catherine was quite lost . . . . She declared that she would give anything in the world to be able to draw; and a lecture on the Picturesque immediately followed, in which his instructions were so clear that she soon began to see beauty in everything admired by him . . . . He talked of foregrounds, distances and second distances; side screens and perspectives; lights and shades; and Catherine was so hopeful a scholar that when they gained the top of Beechen Cliff she voluntarily rejected the whole city of Bath as unworthy to make part of a landscape.

Watercolors had become tremendously popular, and at the turn of the nineteenth century the English public enjoyed the work 83

46. *Fisherman's Cottage,* **by Albert Pinkham Ryder**

47. *A Shady Pool*, by John Sell Cotman

of several superb artists in this medium, who were actively breaking away from preconceived notions of what was, in fact, picturesque. John Sell Cotman (1782–1842) (see Plate 47) was perhaps best known for his quiet, undetailed, and beautifully composed watercolors of scenes that were often the product of his own imagination. Perhaps most interesting is the work of Thomas Girtin (1775–1802). In *The White House* (Plate 48) he almost eliminated details in striving for a gentle atmospheric effect. Girtin's success was so great that many flocked to him for instruction in the art of watercolor. In the 1790's he collaborated with young Joseph Mallord Turner (1775–1851) on landscapes: Girtin made the drawing and Turner added the color. By the time Girtin died, his reputation was so widespread that Turner declared, "If Girtin had lived, I should have starved."

Joseph Turner (1775–1851) and John Constable (1776–1837), almost exact contemporaries, were the greatest landscape painters

48. *The White House,* **by Thomas Girtin**

in England, and possibly the greatest of the romantic age. Constable was born in Suffolk and studied at the Royal Academy. His style, however, took some time to develop, and it was not until he was nearly forty that he began to produce his greatest works. His life was punctuated by frustrations and disappointments. He was not able to marry the woman of his choice until 1816, and she died twelve years later. Ironically, he was appointed a member of the Royal Academy a year after her death, too late, he felt. He became increasingly bitter about the grudging recognition he received, and although this was partly due to his originality, it was also due to his own difficult temperament and biting tongue.

A familiar, intimate countryside appealed to Constable. Early in his life he had loved the Suffolk fields and streams between East Bergholt and Dedham Vale. The masters to whom he turned were the seventeenth-century Dutch painter, Ruisdael, and the English painters, Gainsborough and the more recent Girtin. But Constable introduced new viewpoint and technique.

There were two technical aspects of Constable's art: the sketches in oil or watercolor, and the large, meticulously executed pictures that he sent to the Academy. To many of his contemporaries both were equally horrible. His finished painting entitled *The Hay Wain*, for example, was reviled by some for being unnaturally green, though the same quality, interpreted by others as freshness, led to a rapturous reception from the younger painters in Paris, where, as we have mentioned, Delacroix hastened in response to repaint his *Massacre at Chios*. Constable painstakingly described the structures of vast trees or the mellow russet of brickwork with more vital, brilliant pigment than had previously been seen, and he flooded his canvases with a brilliant, glistening light.

There were times, however, when he disclaimed color and adopted what is called a "limited palette." This was done when he feared that detail might obscure the overall unity of his design. By working very freely on a large scale in a rather muddy brown tone, he was able to discover the unification provided by light and shade. One of his paintings of Salisbury Cathedral (Plate 49) 87

49. *Salisbury Cathedral,* **by John Constable**

serves as a good example of such a work. Archdeacon Fisher was among Constable's closest friends, and it was during visits to him that he made a series of pictures of the cathedral, often as seen over the local streams and meadows.

Constable was said to have been the first painter regularly to take his canvas out of doors. Although, with one unfortunate

exception, he never executed his finished pictures on the spot,
he did in fact make numerous sketches in the open air, famous
for their verve and immediacy. These small sketches are distinguished from the large Academy pictures above all by the
quality of the brushwork. Constable was determined to capture

51. *A View of the Stour,* by John Constable

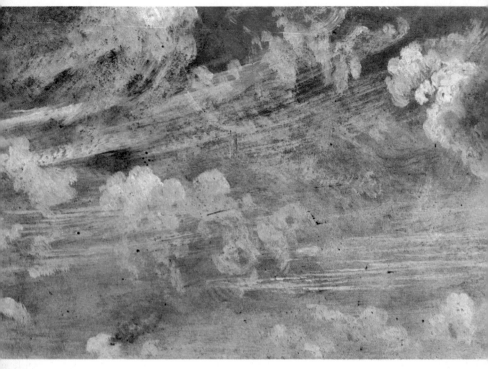

50. *Cloud Study,* **by John Constable**

the essence of a scene before it eluded him. He said that "paint-ing is for me but another word for feeling."

There was a practical advantage, too, in this rapid method of working. He was fascinated by a book by Luke Howard called *The Climate of London,* and he became obsessed with the visual effects of the weather. He made cloud studies (Plate 50), and he wrote to Fisher that the artist "who does not make his skies a material part of his composition is neglecting one of his greatest aids." Many of his sketches, like his briefly executed *A View of the Stour* (Plate 51), are inscribed on the back with cryptic notes on the time of day and the weather. These attempts to pin down

90

the notoriously fickle English climate brought him surprisingly close to the later impressionist painters.

Turner represents a complete contrast to Constable. When Constable visited the Lake District, a region of mountains and lakes in northern England famed for its beauty among artists and writers, his attempts to express the appearance of a mountain shrouded in mist were singularly weak, while it was precisely such scenery that aroused Turner to his greatest imaginative feats. He preferred those moments when nature was most dramatic: iridescent vaporous dawns, blazing sunsets, or the dangerous fury of storms and avalanches. He loved the splendor of the Alps and the shimmering light reflected off the canals and lagoons of Venice. Constable's raindrops rest securely on trees, locked gates, and hedgerows, but Turner's mists dissolve the most obdurate masses in a prismatic light which shimmers, eddies, and curls about the forms.

Turner, unlike Constable, enjoyed tremendous success and considerable recognition early in his career. Although he was the son of a Covent Garden barber, with only a few months of schooling, he began his serious efforts at art before he was ten, exhibiting his first pictures in his father's shop. At fourteen he became a student at the Royal Academy. His early drawings were often tight little topographical views, but their technical excellence was such that at the death of Girtin Turner he was regarded as his artistic heir, and one of the foremost landscapists in England. In 1802 he was elected a member of the Royal Academy. Shortly thereafter, when the signing of the Treaty of Amiens ended the French Revolutionary Wars and made foreign travel possible once more, Turner set out with the express purpose of seeing Napoleon's spectacular loot of art treasures, which were displayed in the Louvre; he then traveled on from Paris to Switzerland, where he stood in rapturous awe before the majesty and splendor of the Alps. The inspiration of foreign travel combined with the security of his position, especially after he was appointed Professor of Perspective at the Academy Schools in 1808, encouraged him to develop his own style with great freedom.

In Turner's finest works his composition is enveloped in an

aura of carmine, chrome yellow, rose madder, ultramarine, cerulean blue, and an indefinable pearly hue. Often these colors were applied as a thin filmy wash over a watercolor. Turner reversed the normal order of things: He melted and dispersed his mountains and imposed a form upon the most intangible substances of all—mist, rain, and snow. In these compositions, the tangible forms would often be suggested by a few touches of dark color, grouped together as a counterpoint to the one shape that haunted Turner, a great curve that has been likened in form to a lasso. For him the whole of nature was drawn into this mysterious vortex, and was radiantly transformed.

Turner's *A View of London from Greenwich* (Plate 52), already bathed in the golden light for which his later works were known, shows the firm foundation upon which his almost abstract creations rested, but he was at his height when he painted the *Burning of the Houses of Parliament* (Plate 53). River and sky are one,

52. *A View of London from Greenwich,* **by J. M. W. Turner**

53. *Burning of the Houses of Parliament,* **by J. M. W. Turner**

54. *Rain, Steam, and Speed—the Great Western Railway,* **by J. M. W. Turner**

united by the moist grayness of air and water and the brilliant plume of flame that flashes across both. All is light—the group of people, the boats in the foreground are less substantial than the fire or its reflection.

In the most "abstract" works of his last days Turner was accused of painting inaccurately; in fact, his paintings were partially accurate; he dissolved the normal visible form into the extraordinary visual effect of light and atmosphere upon it. His painting *Rain, Steam, and Speed* (Plate 54) is a portrait of just those three unsolid elements. When it was first exhibited, it was greeted with derisive howls. Yet there is an amusing story connected with it. One viewer, a young woman, recalled sitting in a train during a storm when an old man opposite her suddenly leaned out of the window. By the time he drew his head back he was drenched with rain, and the young woman, intrigued by anything that could be worth such a soaking, leaned out of the window herself—and was astonished later to see the splendid sight she had witnessed outside that train window immortalized on Turner's canvas.

Turner was a true romantic in that, limited though his education was, he was a passionate lover of poetry, often devising long and complicated poetic titles for his pictures. But although his own writings were not distinguished, the shimmering beauty that invested his visions is very close to what was most sublime in romantic poetry. If we compare Shelley's verses on Venice (from his "Lines Written among the Euganean Hills") with Turner's dreamlike paintings of it (see Plate 55), we shall see that the brush and the printed word have never come more close to the same expression:

> Ocean's nursling, Venice lies,
> A peopled labyrinth of walls,
> Amphitrite's destined halls,
> Which her hoary sire now paves
> With his blue and beaming waves.
> Lo! the sun upsprings behind,
> Broad, red, radiant, half-reclined
> On the level quivering line
> Of the waters crystalline;
> And before that chasm of light,
> As within a furnace bright,
> Column, tower, and dome, and spire,
> Shine like obelisks of fire,
> Pointing with inconstant motion
> From the altar of dark ocean
> To the sapphire-tinted skies;
>
> Those who alone thy towers behold
> Quivering through aëreal gold,
> As I now behold them here,
> Would imagine not they were
> Sepulchres, where human forms,
> Like pollution-nourished worms,
> To the corpse of greatness cling.

95

55. *San Benedetto, Venice,*
by J. M. W. Turner

Realism and the Pre-Raphaelites

THE DEVELOPMENT of realism in the nineteenth century was in a way an outgrowth of romanticism. It, too, was a break with tradition, in this case the tradition of portraying forms of idealized beauty. The realists wanted to convey life as the greater part of humanity saw it—undramatic landscapes, peasants going about their daily tasks, figures from the seamier side of life—the side of life either previously ignored by European painters or charmingly idealized and sentimentalized in small "genre" pictures, as they were called.

Nineteenth-century realism was in some ways the very opposite of romanticism, although it was a result of the romantics' desire to escape into the world of nature and of their exploration of humanity as it really was and not as it was to be presented according to the theories of the classicists. Like romanticism, it was a movement in literature as well as in art.

While in England the serialized installments of Dicken's novels often contained harrowing descriptions of poverty and the life of the lower classes, the true home of realism (and its allied literary movement, naturalism) was France, where Émile Zola and the de Goncourt brothers brought a deep understanding and sympathy to the sufferings of the poor. The de Goncourts's *Germinie Lacerteux,* a novel inspired by their own servant, was published in 1865.

For the roots of nineteenth-century realism we must look to Goya again. His nightmare vision of life at times totally stripped it of artificial beauty or grace. For example, he represented the horror he felt at the atrocities of war in a vast painting of the *Execution of the Insurgents on the 3rd of May 1808* (Plate 56). When Napoleon's army marched into Madrid in the spring of 1808, the nobility stayed indoors, but the people themselves went out to meet the invaders and resist them almost unarmed. The next day came the reprisals; citizens were lined up at the city gate and shot. Here are no colorful uniforms, no horses

56. *Execution of the Insurgents on the 3rd of May, 1808,* by
Francisco José de Goya y Lucientes

with flying manes, no grandiose or heroic poses. A simple
comparison of this picture with Gros's or Géricault's representations of war will sum up much of what is meant by the term "realism." When asked why he painted such scenes, Goya replied,
"To have the pleasure of saying eternally to men that they should
stop being barbarians."

Goya's stark reality found no immediate followers. The next
steps toward realism were taken a generation later, and then in
the field of landscape painting. In the 1830's a group of painters,
led by Théodore Rousseau (1812–1867), went to live in the village

of Barbizon outside Paris. Their move was not a deliberate effort to establish a "school," nor was Barbizon chosen for its spectacular scenery. The country surrounding the village ran to simple farmland—mostly dense orchards and stubbly meadows—that was bordered by forest.

During the early nineteenth century, French landscape painting had fallen somewhat behind that of the English and the Germans. As we have seen, the French were much impressed by *The Hay Wain,* exhibited in Paris in 1824, and although Constable's art did not claim an immediate flurry of followers, his fresh and

57. *A Woodland Stream,* by Constant Troyon

natural color must have lingered in the minds of the painters who settled at Barbizon. In any case, they were determined to take their canvases into the fields and paint nature as it really looked, without even Constable's careful studio reworking of composition. As Rousseau said, "For God's sake . . . let us make a man breathe, a tree really vegetate."

The most impressive area of the nearby countryside was the forest of Fontainebleau, with its splendid, ancient trees. It was the subject for many of the Barbizon painters' works, compositions in shades of green dappled by filtered sunlight. In *A Wood-*

58. *Landscape with Cows,* **by Jules Dupré**

101

59. *A Windy Day,* by Pierre Etienne Théodore Rousseau

land Stream (Plate 57) by Constant Troyon (1810–1865), the artist's use of warm greens, punctuated with russet, gives us a drowsy feeling of midday heat penetrating into the heart of the woods.

Other paintings depict the surroundings of the forest: flat pastures sodden with rain, muddy paths, squelching verges, and cows grazing in waterlogged fields. The Barbizon painters were among the first to recognize the opportunity for startling color offered by fall scenes, as in *Landscape with Cows* (Plate 58) by

Jules Dupré (1811–1889), and capture the strange beauty of late winter days when heavy gray skies offset the colors of the earth. The pale rays of light seen at a distance through the stormy, forbidding atmosphere of Théodore Rousseau's *A Windy Day* (Plate 59) give the viewer a great sense of pathos, although the picture is not without energetic movement, and we almost have a feeling of wind racing over the fields.

These artists found no place for man in their scheme of things; but for Jean François Millet (1814–1875) man occupied a central

103

position. Like Wordsworth in English poetry, Millet in painting introduced the peasant as a revolutionary and a fit subject. Like Wordsworth's characters, too, Millet's peasants have a simple but dignified religion and heroism about them, for both artists shared a moral aim to glorify the hardships and industry of the poor.

This intent was due in part to Millet's background. The son of a peasant farmer, he was born and brought up in a village on the coast of Normandy, a member of a family with a deeply religious strain. At the age of twenty Millet began to train as an artist in Cherbourg, but in 1837 he went to Paris, where he enrolled in the

60. *The Winnower,* **by Jean François Millet**

studio of Paul Delaroche, a highly successful painter of historical and religious subjects in a minutely finished style.

Millet's works of this time reflected the contemporary taste for "pretty" illustration, but when, in 1840, he returned to his native Normandy—he had by this time left Delaroche and had been forced to paint hack portraits and copies of Watteau and Boucher to eke out a living—he produced a series of pictures reflecting humble life in Cherbourg. The desire to record every aspect of a world that he had known since childhood grew stronger and stronger; and although he continued to paint traditional subjects (*St. Jerome* appeared in the Paris Salon of 1845), Millet began to paint, in increasing numbers, pictures such as *The Mother Asking for Alms, The Workman's Monday,* and *The Winnower* (Plate 60).

The Winnower, his balanced study of the struggle of a man grappling with a winnowing basket, was shown at the Paris Salon in 1848 and attracted a good deal of comment, much of it hostile. But Millet had his supporters. One of them, Ledru Rollin, bought the picture for five hundred francs and gave the painter, into the bargain, a commission for a second picture. The money enabled Millet to buy a small cottage at Barbizon, where he lived for the rest of his life.

Once settled in Barbizon, Millet gave up mythological painting almost entirely—in accordance with a vow he made in a letter of 1850—and he concentrated on depicting the world of the poor, from which he himself had emerged, and to which he voluntarily returned. He produced canvases and drawings of patient, weary peasants sowing, harvesting, and leaning on their hoes after hours of unremitting toil. They are sometimes depicted in groups of two or three, bending in unison, or as isolated figures, silhouetted against a low horizon, their feet firmly planted on clods of freshly dug earth. This emphasis of the figures against the sky suggests both the age-old struggle of the laborer and man's determination to vanquish nature. In his painting *Two Peasants Going to Work* (Plate 61), Millet faithfully portrays the exact measure of the peasants' unruffled, purposeful gait.

Millet was less interested in color than were the other Barbizon painters, and he preferred austere forms bounded by a clearly de- 105

61. *Two Peasants Going to Work,* **by Jean François Millet**

fined contour. This may be due to the fact that his early artistic
training consisted of making copies of engravings by Michelangelo
and Poussin. Still, his line is not the hard, smooth line of the
classicists; it is the sketchy, sensitive line with which his contemporary Daumier captured the most fleeting reality. Above all,
Millet's figures, which might have turned out overly sentimental

because of the subjects he depicts, are instead grandly monumental and eternal. Despite the fact that Millet himself wanted his peasants to look "so that imagination cannot conceive of their ever being anything else," the woman in his *Peasant Woman Baking Bread* might be some primeval goddess going about a cosmic task.

The name of Jean Baptiste Camille Corot (1796–1875) is one of the best known of those associated with the Barbizon school, although he was a constant traveler and of all the painters of that school the least closely linked with the actual village community. Corot was born in Paris, the son of successful milliners. His mother was court *modiste* to Napoleon I, and he himself was destined by his parents for the trade of draper, but he rebelled and at the age of twenty-six took up painting. He studied under two classical landscape painters and three years later, in 1825, set out for Italy.

This visit was the turning point in his career. With the memory of those works of Constable's that he had seen in Paris still fresh, he spent most of his time painting out of doors, in the streets of Rome or in the torrid countryside surrounding the city. Noticing how every shrub and boulder stood out against the sunbaked earth with unnatural clarity, he realized that to achieve the effect he wanted he would have to organize and simplify the forms and tones of his pictures. He learned how to place unfalteringly the single accent of color that would bring the whole view into focus. As he said, "There must be no indecision in anything." He made small sketches, carried out on the spot, of little towns and villages clinging precariously to the rock hillsides. In *The Bridge at Narni* (Plate 62), he makes the eye leap with the agility of a mountain goat from shrub to boulder and across the excitingly complex surfaces of what might otherwise be rather dull hillsides. He later sent to the Salon a version of this scene that was more elaborate, but disappointingly tame. By contrast to the vibrant, original *The Bridge at Narni,* in *View of the Colosseum* (Plate 63), he uses more somber tones to conjure up the desolation as evening falls, while his bold brushstrokes contribute to the starkness of the mood.

62. *The Bridge at Narni,* by Jean Baptiste Camille Corot

63. *View of the Colosseum,* by Jean Baptiste Camille Corot

Corot was a kindly, modest, and unassuming person. He was successful, and never lacking for money, which he gave generously to Millet's widow when she was in need, and also to Daumier in his blind old age. In 1846 he was presented with the Legion of Honor. It was in the 1840's that he realized his kinship with the painters of the Barbizon school and began to concentrate on the landscape of France. Still, he remained a traveler, visiting Italy, Holland, Switzerland, and England when he was not traveling throughout France. These visits were always made during the summer, when he could sketch out of doors. In the winter he worked in his studio, creating larger, more elaborate pictures for the Salon, but on the whole, like Constable, he needed the presence of the landscape before him to release his imagination, and the pictures he painted in winter were often tame and correctly dull, even though they were almost invariably well designed.

Around 1850 a radical change took place in Corot's style. He began to paint pictures like his *Gust of Wind*, bathed in a blurry, silvery light that suggested a poetic, sunless afternoon or twilight. This was due partly to the influence of early photography, with its restricted range of tones and fusing of images. Perhaps the new technique was most successful in his portraits, which are superb, though often overlooked.

Corot's wistful *A Girl Doing Her Hair* (Plate 64) is executed in the cool tones of filtered light and with the softer, more sensitive modeling of his later style. Corot had been painting figure studies since the very beginning of his career, and as he grew older, he attached more and more importance to them. Like the impressionists, whom he influenced in this respect, he always liked to have what he was painting directly in front of him, and during winter, when he kept to his Paris studio and was denied scenery, he continued his habit of painting from life by having models pose for him. He exhibited two of these figure paintings, but they did not please the public. Corot was by nature timid and did not try to show them again. Today they are among the most prized of his works.

When Corot died in 1875, the impressionist movement was already established. Earlier he had encouraged the impres- 109

64. *A Girl Doing Her Hair,* by Jean Baptiste Camille Corot

sionists with such words as, "Always be true to your first impression. . . ," and in extreme old age he was himself influenced by these brilliant young artists.

Gustave Courbet (1819–1877), who gave the movement of realism its name, was born at Ornans in the Franche-Comté. Like Corot, Courbet had to overcome strong paternal resistance before he could become an artist. His father, Régis Courbet, was a rich and respected farmer who wished his son to enter upon a legal career. In fact, nobody could have been less suited to such a profession. Courbet had no scholastic abilities and had been the despair of his Jesuit schoolmasters.

Eventually his father agreed to allow him to paint, provided him with a modest income, and sent him to Paris. Once there, Courbet refused to enter any of the recognized establishments for the training of artists. Instead he spent long hours in the Louvre, and in a very real sense his masters were the great painters of the sixteenth and seventeenth centuries, especially the Venetians and the Dutch—so his proud boast that he was self-taught was not literally true.

His first successful picture was a self-portrait in which he endowed himself with a certain romantic charm. Even when he was very stout and middle-aged, Courbet was still guilty of the most unashamed conceit. He also loved to brag about his physical strength. It was perhaps because of his arrogant animal spirits that he concentrated so on solidity in his paintings. The same quality that gave him an insatiable appetite for life gave to his pictures such physical power that one feels he could sink his teeth into Courbet's apples or grasp his women round the waist.

Courbet made his debut in the Salon in 1844, but perhaps the most important year of his life was 1849, when he made friends with Corot and came to know Baudelaire, the poet, and the thinker and writer, Pierre Joseph Proudhon. It was Proudhon's theories of the aim of the painter that best summed up Courbet's object and his works: "The art of painting should consist only in the representation of objects which the artist can see and touch. . . . Painting is essentially a concrete art and can only consist of the representation of real and existing things. It is a completely 111 physical language which is made up not of words but of all visible objects." These ideas are very far from those of Blake. "Show me an angel," said Courbet, "and I will paint one."

Paintings like Courbet's *The Winnowers* (Plate 65) shocked the public because they revealed the dull and backbreaking monotony of the peasants' tasks without even Millet's touch of sentiment. Courbet portrayed reality simply as it might look in a camera—a stone breaker in his dust-covered overalls, with holes in his socks, or the painter himself strolling on a hot day in his shirt sleeves— with as little philosophic reflection as possible.

In *The Winnowers* the structure of the barn is curiously vague. Courbet could never quite grasp the representation of interior space. Technically he was more successful with landscapes, and it is only in paintings like *Deer in a Forest Clearing* (Plate 66) that he was the least bit sentimental.

From 1850 onward Courbet found himself at loggerheads with the official guardians of taste. In 1855 *The Studio* (detail) (Plate 67), which he wished to exhibit at Paris's Exposition Universelle, was rejected by the exposition judges. In this picture Courbet appears in the center of his studio painting a landscape, while a model, draped only in a sheet, stands peering over his shoulder like a kind of realist muse and a strange, motley assemblage of people hover about the room, all recognizable friends and acquaintances of the artist. The picture was incomprehensible to classicists and romanticists alike, and it was as a result of his anger at the general disapprobation he had met with that Courbet published a manifesto proclaiming his ideas and opened a one-man exhibition entitled simply, "Realism, G. Courbet."

Courbet's technique, like his forms, was solid and direct. His color was frequently thickly applied and the greens especially were very vivid. It was opaque, because he reverted to the seventeenth-century practice of "priming," or covering the canvas with an undercoat of dark paint. His technical innovations were most striking in his landscapes. In order to depict the chalk face of the Franche-Comté hills, he would load his palette knife with thick, whitish gray pigment and apply it directly to the canvas, 112 creating great layers of paint that seem to symbolize the harsh

66. *Deer in a Forest Clearing,* **by Gustave Courbet**

surface of the cliffs. Courbet never cared for insubstantial or
fleeting effects. He depicted even the ocean (Plate 68) as something almost solid.

In 1871 disaster overcame Courbet. During the Commune, the
government of the Parisian insurrection that followed the Franco-

65. *The Winnowers*, by Gustave Courbet

Prussian War, he was nominated *Président des Artistes*. Despite his efforts to protect the Louvre from fire, he was arrested on June 7th and charged with giving the order for the destruction of the Vendôme Column, a Parisian monument of substantial importance. He probably had nothing to do with it. Although he was finally released, his goods were seized in the following year, and he went into voluntary exile in Switzerland, where he died, depressed and homesick, five years later.

Unlike the Barbizon painters, whom he counted among his friends, Honoré Daumier (1808–1879) was totally indifferent to landscape. His life was spent in Paris, and his subjects were the forms and faces of the Paris masses and the foibles of society. His art depended on the quickness of his eye, which allowed no characteristic gesture, action, or expression escape him. He was perhaps the only caricaturist who was also a great painter.

Daumier's father was an indigent picture framer who longed in vain to become a poet. As a result of his poverty Daumier's education was cut short, and at the age of twelve he was forced to take on odd jobs, working first for a bailiff and then for a bookseller. Later in his life he was to translate the kind of scenes he had witnessed in his youth into art, to produce lacerating pictures of French lawyers and of rodentlike amateur print collectors burrowing among portfolios, their thin noses twitching with excitement as they think they may have discovered a masterpiece. But Daumier's inquisitive eye also recorded children let out of school and other everyday themes, like his timeless, weary Washerwoman, her exhausted bulk outlined against the glare of the river bank.

For much of Daumier's life he was a graphic artist. The technique of lithography had recently been invented, affording artists a new method of reproduction whereby a drawing could be made directly on the stone printing block by the use of a specially prepared grease-containing ink or crayon. Goya, Delacroix, and Géricault had all experimented with this new medium, which provided a constant outlet for Daumier's talents. After a five-year apprenticeship in the workshop of a printer, he began to make a name for himself as a cartoonist and satirist in the press. He   115

67. *The Studio* (detail), by Gustave Courbet

68. *The Sea*, by Gustave Courbet

lampooned the corruption of law and government with so swift and unerring a line that, as the result of one of his drawings, a portrayal of Louis Philippe as Gargantua, he found himself imprisoned for six months.

Daumier's brilliant caricatures earned him far more popular acclaim than did his paintings. It was during the unsettled years after 1852, when Louis Napoleon had seized power, that Daumier began to paint in earnest. But the constant drudgery of having to produce as many as three drawings a week for the press meant that he had to fit in his painting when and where he could. Moreover, the habits of the caricaturist were so ingrained that the qualities of his drawings were transferred onto the canvas, and he used his brush as he had used his pen. Daumier depicted vividly lawyers (whom he regarded as tricksters) talking to their frightened, awkward clients before a hearing, or drinkers raptly gratifying their thirst; and the rhythms of his cursive, heavily loaded brushstrokes seem to correspond to the rhythmic gulps of the drinkers or the suspenseful pause in a game of chess as the players reflect on their next moves. In *The Chess Players* (Plate 69) Daumier shows his rare psychological insight and manages to convey the secret pondering of one player and the nervous tension of the other.

The Drama (Plate 70) exemplifies the strengths and weaknesses of Daumier's painting. As ever, it is Daumier's brilliant and sensitive line that captures the scene—the audience, aghast, and the gesture of despair on the stage. Did she kill him? Did she drive him to suicide? It is, in any case a drama. The painting is also a caricature. Moreover, Daumier was so used to working in black and white that, although he uses the dark and light of a theater skillfully, there is hardly any use of color. Nor does the painting seem quite finished. But then Daumier always found the act of painting difficult. In his journal entry for February 5, 1849, Delacroix records that the poet and critic Baudelaire had just paid him a visit. "He told me," he writes, "of the difficulties which Daumier experiences in finishing."

The movement toward realism in nineteenth-century painting

69. *The Chess Players,* by Honore Daumier

70. *The Drama*, by
Honoré Daumier

was not restricted to France alone, although it enjoyed its first and most important flowering there. In Germany, Wilhelm Leibl (1844–1900) was much influenced by Courbet, whom he met at the Munich International Exhibition in 1869, but he was obviously influenced, too, by Holbein and Dürer. Leibl was seeking to depict realistic subject matter with the technical perfection of those earlier masters when he produced his most famous work, *Three Peasant Women in a Village Church* (Plate 71). It took four years to paint and was executed with meticulous truth, much of the work being done on the spot. As he wrote to his mother:

> It really takes great staying power to bring such a difficult, detailed picture to completion in the circumstances. Most of the time I have literally taken my life into my hands in order to paint it. For up to now the church has been as cold as the grave, so that one's fingers get completely stiff. Sometimes, too, it is so dark that I have the greatest difficulty in getting a clear enough view of the part on which I am working. . . . I have been having very bad luck with the picture. For instance, I could not finish the hands of the last figure, because when I had already got a long way with them the model developed a boil and an inflammation of the eye, so that I could not finish the head either.

He was interested not only in painting the ostensible subject, three women in church, but also in depicting such things as wood, stone, cloth.

American painting always tended toward realistic subject matter, but perhaps the most deliberate exponent of painting straight from nature was Winslow Homer (1836–1910), who maintained that "if a man wants to be an artist, he must never look at pictures." He said, "You must wait, and wait patiently, until the exceptional, the wonderful effect or aspect comes." "I work very hard every afternoon from 4:30 to 4:40, that being the limit of the light that I represent—the title of my picture being *Early Evening.*" Although famous for his seascapes and paintings of the fisherfolk of his native New England, Homer, in *Croquet* (Plate 72), interprets the exact feeling of a mid-afternoon lawn party in a way that Courbet would have approved.

71. *Three Peasant Women in a Village Church,* by **Wilhelm
Leibl**

72. *Croquet,* **by Winslow Homer**

Millet once wrote, "Art began to decline from the moment that the artist did not lean directly and naively upon impressions made by nature. Cleverness naturally and rapidly took the place of nature, and decadence then began. . . . At the bottom it always comes to this: a man must be moved himself in order to move others, and all that is done from theory, however clever, can never attain this end, for it is impossible that it should have the breath of life." This summed up the aims of the painters of the school of nineteenth-century realism. It was also the core of the belief of a group of painters in England who called themselves pre-Raphaelites. But in their case, although the basic feeling was the same, the results were very different.

Pre-Raphaelite painting appeared in England in the middle of the century. All over Europe 1848 had been a year of revolution, of threat to established orders of every kind. In England on the tenth of April of that year the Chartists, members of a movement seeking to democratize further the British electoral system, assembled to march into London and present their petition to Parliament. Violence was feared; Queen Victoria had left the capital, and the military was ready. Among the crowd were two young artists whose purposes, equally revolutionary, were in a different sphere. William Holman Hunt (1827–1910) and John Everett Millais (1829–1896) were youthfully determined to overthrow what they saw as the tyrannical stranglehold of the Royal Academy on the progress of English art. They felt that the accepted methods of the painters who were their elders were stultifying and dully repetitive, and that to follow the conventions sanctioned by the Academy would be death to the freshness and sincerity of their own art. In particular, they disliked Raphael's *Transfiguration*; it was a work in which they could see only pompous attitudinizing or posing; the grandeur of its style seemed empty; it ignored the simplicity of nature and of truth. And since Raphael's time, they felt, the conventional tradition of painting had been one of repetitious banality and insincerity of feeling. In Millais's cramped studio in Gower Street they plotted their own revolution—an adjustment of the whole course of European painting by means of a return to the fidelity and purpose, more than the forms, of painting before the High Renaissance. And thus it was that they came to be known as "pre-Raphaelites."

Hunt and Millais were soon joined by Dante Gabriel Rossetti (1828–1882) and several others. Rossetti was a man of half a dozen worlds—a painter, poet, worldly joker, and gloriously free Bohemian. It has been said that of these painters Rossetti was the dreamer, the real romantic of the group; Holman Hunt, with his fervent religious paintings, its conscience; and Millais, its brightest star.

It may seem strange that a member of a movement so close to realism should be called a romantic, but this is because the pre-Raphaelites took something from both movements. They chose lofty, often romantic, subject matter, as far from everyday life as possible—themes from literature, history, and the Bible—which they then treated with the utmost realism. The result was 125 such that Charles Dickens furiously denounced Millais's *Christ in the House of His Parents* because it had dared to show the Holy Family as ordinary living people. Hunt, in his painting entitled *Shadow of Death* (Plate 73), has perhaps been too literal in his attempt to represent Christ's carpenter shop down to its last wood shaving and its implausibly modern-looking equipment. *The Washing of the Feet* (Plate 74), by Ford Maddox Brown (1821–1893), another member of the movement, depicts Christ washing the feet of St. Peter with such realistic detail that Peter's sandals are almost embarrassingly shabby.

In the case of Millais's *Ophelia* (Plate 75), the painting of the pallid body, icy water, and almost photographic foliage is technically superb, but the pre-Raphaelite combination of exotic subject matter and realistic treatment results in an effect that is simply alarming. Rossetti's painting (Plate 76) entitled *Beata Beatrix* ("Blessed Beatrice") in memory of his wife is altogether more romantic. The painter identifies his personal feeling with that of Dante's idealized feeling for his beloved Beatrice, creating a dreamlike vision of shadowy figures and warm light that strongly suggests longing for the lost, although in this case the sentiment is too extreme.

The pre-Raphaelites were met at first with a barrage of abuse, but this did not last, and they soon enjoyed considerable success. Hunt won a prize from the Liverpool Academy, and Millais was elected an Associate of the Royal Academy. With the exception of the great portraitist, Sir Thomas Lawrence, Millais was the youngest painter ever to be so honored. A large part of this change of public opinion was due to the intervention of John Ruskin, the foremost critic of the day. He used his personal influence and powers of persuasion in letters to the London *Times,* and in a pamphlet that argued that these painters, despite their youth and inexperience, despite the faults that were admittedly present in their works, had nevertheless produced pictures of power and beauty. In any case, the pre-Raphaelites' approach to traditional subject matter was completely original, their color was fresh and bright, and they stood staunchly against the general hideousness and destruction of beauty that the Industrial Revolu-

73. *Shadow of Death*, by William Holman Hunt

74. *The Washing of the Feet,* by Ford Maddox Brown

75. *Ophelia*, **by John Everett Millais**

tion had brought to England, its towns and its countryside, in the nineteenth century.

John Ruskin's admiration for medieval architecture contributed to the romantic equivalent of the classical revival—the Gothic revival. The romantic escapism that attracted the French to the gory lion hunts of Delacroix and the *Orientales* of Hugo led the English to muse on the misty ruins of the Middle Ages. Thus it was that Scott wrote *The Lady of the Lake* based on Scotland's past and Keats, the richly medieval *The Eve of St. Agnes;* "Gothic" tales abounded, while medieval "monasteries," churches, and castles were recreated with the help of papier-mâché and plaster all over England. Not that the creators of nineteenth-century 129

76. *Beata Beatrix*, by Dante Gabriel Rossetti

Neo-Gothic architecture lacked in earnestness. They studied Gothic structures with scientific intensity to be sure that their copied decoration was in every way correct. Probably the Houses of Parliament (Plate 77), reconstructed in Gothic style after the fire in 1834, are their proudest achievement. The work of two architects, Sir Charles Barry (1795–1860) and Augustus W. N. Pugin (1812–1852), the Houses combined Gothic detail with more

77. The Houses of Parliament, London, designed by Charles Barry and A. W. N. Pugin

78. The Opera, Paris, designed by Jean Louis Charles Garnier

contemporary plan and proportions. In any case the result was successful, and seen through a twilight fog, the Houses of Parliament suggest all the romance of a Scott novel and also the dignity of a parliamentary government that had its roots in the medieval past.

In general, nineteenth-century architects attempted to duplicate every style they knew from the past. Architectural textbooks were rifled to produce buildings like the birthday-cake baroque of the Paris Opera (Plate 78), designed by Jean Louis Charles Garnier (1825–1898), or the more austere late-Renaissance Burg Theater (Plate 79) in Vienna, the work of Gottfried Semper (1803–1879) and Karl von Hasenanex (1833–1894).

Meanwhile, because of the new demands of the industrial age
132 and an expanding society, new forms came to be required, for

79. The Burg Theater, Vienna, designed by Gottfried Semper
and Karl von Hasenanex

80. The Hothouse, Kew Gardens, London, designed by Decimus
Burton and Richard Turner

which there were no historical precedents. It was at this time that architects began to use iron as a basic part of the structure of buildings. Greenhouses and conservatories were among the first buildings to depend on iron and glass. The huge hothouse at Kew Gardens (Plate 80) just outside London, designed by Decimus Burton and Richard Turner, is a remarkable example with its delicate curve of iron ribbing. When Henri Labrouste (1801–1875) designed the National Library (Plate 81) in Paris, the first French library to be designed as an individual building, he boldly and decoratively used a metal framework exposed to view. These structures marked the beginning of truly functional architecture.

81. The National Library: Reading Room, Paris, designed by Henri Labrouste

Impressionism

THE NINETEETH CENTURY had seen the freed composition and brisk brushwork of Géricault and Delacroix, the fresh light and color of Constable and the Barbizon painters, the mistily suggested forms of Turner. The stage was now set for impressionism.

The impressionists were a group of young painters (Edouard Manet [1832–1883], their senior member, was thirteen years younger than Courbet) who carried their experiments with the portrayal of visual reality beyond anything that had been done before. They were a group in that they were friends, they frequently painted together, they exhibited together, and they were castigated together. Their chief interest was light.

The impressionists felt that the glorious brilliance of true sunlight had never in fact been painted, not even by the master Turner, whom they greatly admired. Light, as well as motion, they noticed, obscured details, which the painter frequently included in his work although they could not possibly be captured by a glance at the actual scene. In nature many flecks of color converge upon the eye and are translated into a definite shape. The impressionists tried to recreate this process in their painting. They noticed that nature provides the eye with few outlines, that shadows are not merely darker shades of what is illuminated but are themselves full of reflected light. All these discoveries were revolutionary.

Almost twenty years passed between Courbet's exhibition of "realism" and the first impressionist showing, which was held in the abandoned studio of the photographer Nadar in 1874. They were years of enormous change. France had suffered complete economic collapse with her defeat in the Franco-Prussian War, and the Civil War had reshaped the United States. Two scientific advances had enormously extended man's ability both to destroy and to save life: Nobel had discovered the explosive powers of nitroglycerine, and five years later, in 1867, Lister had introduced antiseptics into surgery. In 1859 Darwin had published his *Origin* 135

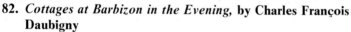

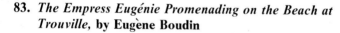

82. *Cottages at Barbizon in the Evening,* **by Charles François Daubigny**

83. *The Empress Eugénie Promenading on the Beach at Trouville,* **by Eugène Boudin**

of Species. These events had struck, respectively, at the roots of the established order of belief and at the balance of political power.

Meanwhile the impressionists had been working out their theories. Two scientific innovations particularly affected them. One was the development of photography—and the consequences for art can well be imagined. The expensive and laborious process of portrait painting was no longer needed, and was therefore no longer a source of income for the artist. The painter could not compete with the photographer, but he could attempt to portray a heightened reality that was beyond the grasp of his rival's camera. The other innovation affecting the impressionists was the development of the theory of complementary color, which had

been evolved by the chemist Chevreul, director of the Gobelins tapestry works, in 1839. This provided a scientific basis for the impressionists' use of touches of pure primary colors—red, blue, and yellow—and of their complementaries—green, orange, and purple—in a revolutionary way. At the same time the impressionists absorbed the influence and advice of their elders, Corot and Courbet, and of the lesser-known Eugene Boudin (1824–1898) (see Plate 83) and Charles François Daubigny (1817–1878) (see Plate 82), the latter of whom as a close friend of the Barbizon painters. Both Boudin, who was known for his bright, gusty seaside paintings, and Daubigny had a fresh free approach which the impressionists admired.

A study of the great impressionists one by one will give us some 137 idea of their movement and the breadth of their discoveries. Edouard Manet was the most outstanding of them all in that he was the earliest, in his time, and the best known. The son of a well-to-do father, Manet was from the very beginning a person of eminence. He studied at the studio of Couture, a successful Parisian artist, but Manet's independence often outraged his academic master. He first attracted the attention of the public with a series of canvases inspired by a troupe of Spanish dancers who were delighting Parisian audiences. From the very first his unusual use of color disturbed the critics. One wrote that Manet's was "a caricature of color, not color itself."

At this time Manet was not an impressionist, but rather a realist in the style of Courbet, and yet in carrying his realism one step further than Courbet, he aroused the public ire. In 1863 more than four thousand works were rejected by the Salon jury, and Emperor Louis Napoleon, in response to violent protests, ordered that there be a show of the rejected pictures. The result was the now-famous Salon of the Rejected or *Salon des Refusés.* It was regarded as a great joke, but special scorn was reserved for the works of Manet, especially his *Breakfast on the Grass* (Plate 84). The Emperor pronounced it "immodest," and the Empress, deeply embarassed, looked the other way. What was the object of all this dismay? A painting of a female nude seated on the grass with two fully dressed men, a picnic basket and its contents beside them, with another figure knee-deep in the river beyond. But in this case the nude was not the kind of idealized goddess to which the Salon visitors were accustomed—she was a very real-looking woman of Paris, with the air of an artist's model, and her companions were dressed, like the figures in Courbet's or Daumier's paintings, in the fashions of the day. Oddly enough, this very shocking piece of realism was based on two great works of the Renaissance. One was the *Concert Champêtre* by Giorgione, a painting in which a lavishly dressed courtier of Giorgione's period, strumming a lute, is joined by another male companion and two nude nymphs. The other, from which Manet drew the composition of his picture, was a little-known engraving by Marc Antonio Raimondi after a painting by Raphael entitled *Neptune and Nymphs.* Manet

138

84. *Breakfast on the Grass,* **by Edouard Manet**

had studied both of these works during the many hours he had
spent in the Louvre.

Apart from its subject, there was something else disturbing
about Manet's painting—his new treatment of the figures. There
is no surface gloss to the picture, and the tones must have seemed

flat to the critics of the day. There is little shadow, and the light does not appear to have come from any likely source. Yet there is an "open air" feeling about the painting.

Moreover Manet's style was to develop further. He had become friendly with a group of young painters who were in the vanguard of impressionism, and he spent much time engaged in lengthy discussions with them at the Café Guerbois. As a result of his contact with their ideas Manet's technique became softer, his contours less sharply defined, and his tones lighter and less harshly contrasted. For a brief period in the mid-1870's he painted at the riverside town of Argenteuil with Claude Monet (1840–1926), the young man who had undertaken most seriously to exemplify in his works the theories of the impressionists. Monet always painted in the open air, and on the advice of Daubigny, he had constructed for himself a studio-boat, so that he could be closer to the myriad reflections of river scenery. Manet, as a tribute to the young artist, painted a picture of Monet at work in his floating studio (Plate 85). The picture is a tribute in style as well as subject. Here Manet uses the brilliant color and brief free brush-strokes of impressionism to get the effect of a glance at the sunlit scene. His method of capturing the momentary look of things is perhaps best summed up in a letter he wrote to the author Marcel Proust, whose portrait he exhibited in the Salon of 1880:

> For the last three weeks, my dear friend, your portrait has been in the Salon, badly hung on a piece of wall next to a door, and still more badly spoken of. Still, it is my lot to be abused, and I take it philosophically. Ah! the portrait with the hat, where everything, people said, was blue! Well, I'm biding my time. I shall not see that day myself. But after my death people will realize that I saw things correctly and had the right ideas. Your portrait is an outstandingly sincere work. I remember as though it were yesterday the rapid, summary fashion in which I dealt with the glove of the ungloved hand. And when you said to me, at that very moment, "Please, not another touch," I felt we were so perfectly attuned. . . .

Although Manet's name will always be associated with the im-
140 pressionists, he never wanted to run the risk of following their

85. *Monet Painting in his Floating Studio,* **by Edouard Manet**

86. *The Bar of the Folies-Bergère,* **by Edouard Manet**

ideas to the point of losing his sense of solid form or the effects of a firm outline, and a strong composition. In his later years he was able cleverly to combine the virtues of his earlier style with a marvelous, light impressionism. His painting of *The Bar of the Folies-Bergère* (Plate 86) is a superb example. It was Manet's last major painting, and was executed in 1881. (The previous

year he had suffered a crippling illness that made it hard to sustain the kind of long effort and enthusiasm required by such a picture.) Before the viewer stands the barmaid, as if about to take an order. Behind her is a mirror that reflects not only the barmaid herself and her customer, but also the entire audience at the Folies-Bergère. The painter has deliberately altered the relationship be-

143

tween the actual objects and their reflection in a further exploration of a scene he has already presented frontally. Despite this somewhat jarring visual note, the total, momentary effect of glittering chandeliers, orbs of light, and the motley, noisy crowd in evening dress is overpowering.

Claude Monet was, of all the impressionists, the truest to their ideas. He was born in Paris in 1840, the son of a druggist, and when he was still a child, his family moved to Le Havre. At sixteen his interest in art was such that he was sent to study with a local master. It was at this time that he met, and came to admire the work of Boudin, who persuaded him, despite Monet's great reluctance, to join him on an outdoor painting expedition. Later Monet excitedly described what had happened on that outing: "It was as if a veil had suddenly been torn from my eyes. I understood. I grasped what painting was capable of being."

From that moment on he was determined to be a landscape painter, and three years later, when he was nineteen, he came closer to his ambition. He left Le Havre for Paris, where he met and admired the Barbizon painter Troyon. Much to his parents' chagrin, he refused either to come home or to attend the École des Beaux-Arts (School of Fine Arts), and as a result they cut his allowance.

During the 1860's Monet slowly developed his own style. An early example is his *Breakfast on the Grass* (Plate 87), called "The Picnic," a painting far more revolutionary in treatment, if not in subject matter, than Manet's painting by the same name. The dress of the woman in the foreground is only barely sketched in; the tree above her head consists of mere daubs of color. If we are to believe the painter, the man's suit is of the darkest blue, but is pale blue at the shoulder. Certainly lights and shadows had never been depicted in this fashion before, and yet the effect of intense noonday sun glimmering here and there through trees had never been more successfully achieved.

Despite the novelty and independence of his approach, Monet enjoyed tremendously the company and valued the advice of other painters. In 1863 he stayed with Pierre Auguste Renoir 144 and the Englishman Alfred Sisley, both impressionists, in the

87. *Breakfast on the Grass* (detail), by Claude Monet

88. *La Grenouillère,* **by Claude Monet**

Forest of Fontainebleau, where he watched Delacroix from a
friend's window as the aged master painted in his garden studio.
Two years later he joined Courbet and Daubigny at Trouville,
where he met the young American so interested in the impressionist movement, James Abbott McNeill Whistler. In 1869, he
painted with Renoir at La Grenouillère, a popular restaurant and
bathing place that has often been regarded as the birthplace of
impressionism. Though his picture of it (Plate 88) was not yet
"impressionistic" in the full sense of the word, Monet's bold
strokes of gold and turquoise conjured up the agitated ripples of
water in an entirely novel way. He had observed that the sunlight,
reflected by the trees on the far side, was again reflected in the
wavelets over the entire surface of the river.

146

The mood of Monet's paintings is so light and gay that it is hard to imagine he was in such despair that he had been driven to attempt suicide. In fact, Monet was constantly struggling with desperate poverty and was often saved only by the timely aid of his friends, Courbet and Renoir among others. On one occasion Renoir stole bread from his mother's table in order to prevent Monet and his little family from starving. He was sometimes forced by his poverty to use the same canvas twice, which made it difficult for him to keep his tones clear. His works were rejected for the Salon of 1870, and he wrote in despair to a friend:

> Gaudibert has again had the goodness to make it possible for me to settle here and to bring back my little family. Now we are settled and I am in very good fettle and full of the will to work, but alas, that fatal rejection is almost taking the bread out of my mouth, and in spite of my moderate prices, dealers and collectors turn their backs on me. It is particularly depressing to see how little interest is taken in any work of art that is not in public favor.

Two journeys had a decided effect on Monet's art. The first was made during his military service, when he was stationed in North Africa—he never forgot its light and color. The second was at the time of the Franco-Prussian War, when he and Camille Pissarro (1830–1903) fled to England. Corot probably encouraged him to study the works of Constable, and, in addition, although Monet claimed to dislike Turner because of his choice of elaborate literary titles for his paintings, Turner's works must have exerted a strong influence on him. It was shortly after this that he painted a picture called *Impression: Sunrise,* from which the impressionist movement got it name.

It was shown at an exhibition which Monet and a group of his friends, discouraged by their rejection from the Salon, organized independently in 1874. Among those who exhibited along with Monet were Renoir, Sisley, Pissarro, Edgar Degas (1834–1917), and Paul Cézanne (1839–1906). The public howled, and a carping critic, noting the name of one of Monet's canvases, jeeringly called the entire group "impressionists," a name which soon enough lost its insulting flavor.

Some two years later Monet painted *The Gare St.-Lazare,* an example of the impressionist's willingness to take any subject and turn it into a pattern of vibrant color. Monet's fleeting "impression" of the station, its puffs of steam and the handsome structure of the shed blurred by the thick mist within, is scarcely less beautiful than the most lovely landscape. He painted ten pictures of this railway station, and they marked the beginning of his habit of making prolonged studies of a single subject. He did a series of haystacks, and a number of pictures of Rouen Cathedral (see Plate 89), which he viewed from a window opposite its portal. That these subjects should be so varied is not really surprising, as, with most impressionist works, the true subject of any painting is light, falling upon varied surfaces.

Monet's paintings of Rouen Cathedral are among his greatest works, and nothing could be further from the neat precision of the "picturesque" watercolors popular at the time. When the pictures are seen in succession, the vast and complicated facade literally dissolves with the changing light into a lacelike mist and the cathedral has the ethereal appearance the original architects must have intended.

Monet concentrated more than any painter before or since on the truth of Delacroix's words, "When the tones are right, the lines draw themselves." In all his works he was particularly concerned with the transformation of objects brought about by the daily course of the sun. So anxious was he to capture the immediate impression of a scene that he was driven to desperation by the quite natural changes that take place from day to day. Once, while painting a river view, he wrote to a friend:

Never have I been so unlucky with the weather. Never three suitable days in succession, so I have to be always making changes, for everything is growing and turning green. And I had dreamt of painting the Creuse just as we saw it! In short, by dint of changes, I am following Nature without being able to grasp her, and then there is the river that shrinks, swells again, green one day, then yellow, sometimes almost dry, and which tomorrow will be a torrent, after the terrible rain that is falling at the moment . . . .

89. *The Facade of Rouen Cathedral,* **by Claude Monet**

One can well imagine him furiously painting the face of Rouen Cathedral as the moving sun threw first one series of shadows and then another across it.

The chief delight of Monet's declining years was the water-lily   149

garden he had built at Giverny, where he settled, and from 1912 until his death he devoted himself almost exclusively to painting it. By now he was lonely, disagreeable, and increasingly self-critical, liable to destroy any painting which failed to satisfy him. Frequently the water-lily pool or *nymphéas* pictures (see Plate 90) are highly decorative, and their design reminds us of his lifelong passion for Japanese prints, which he collected for many years. These pools are poetically beautiful, and yet almost "abstract." The surface is reduced to rippling strands and whirls of translucent paint, which is often so thin that it begins to spread and run down the canvas.

When Hilaire Germain Edgar Degas (1834–1917), son of a wealthy banker and a New Orleans-born Creole mother, was twenty, he gave up his legal studies and became an artist. At this point he had a chance meeting with Ingres that was to determine the entire future course of his work. On learning Degas was to take up painting, the aged master urged him to "draw lines, young man, many lines; from memory or from nature. It is in this way that you will become a good artist." It was Ingres's advice that prevented Degas from ever being a true impressionist, although he exhibited with the impressionists and was much interested in their

90. *Les Nymphéas,* by Claude Monet

ideas. He entered the École des Beaux-Arts and the following year set out for Italy, determined to study the Italian painters whom he had always admired, as well as the works of antiquity. He was glad to leave behind him the Parisian artistic environment, which already bored and disgusted him, and he wrote in his notebook: "It seems to me today, if one wants to engage seriously in art . . . it is necessary to steep oneself again in solitude." Though Degas was an urbane and sophisticated man, his relations with his fellow artists were always precarious for he was also irritable, sensitive, and arrogant, and he became, in later life, a fussy bachelor who was perpetually fretting about his health. During his visit to Italy he painted his aunt, Baroness Bellelli, and her family in their home in Florence (Plate 91). They make a beautiful but curious group; the strong outline and the smooth modeling of the heads betray Degas's admiration for Ingres and Raphael, while the unconventional grouping was perhaps inspired by Courbet.

Shortly after Degas's return to Paris, he met Manet in the Louvre; they recognized immediately that they had many ideas in common and became firm friends. At this time (around 1860), however, there was much in Degas's art which Manet must have found distasteful, especially his use of historical themes. But   151

Degas gradually discovered where his true interest lay, and applied himself to the recording of strangely familiar and seemingly unpromising subjects: milliners, ballet dancers practicing, washerwomen, and dejected drinkers in cafés, as in his painting *The Absinthe Drinkers* (Plate 92). Unlike that of Monet, Degas's subject matter was humanity, and he never for a moment lost his sense of line, which was as brilliant and telling in characterizing his subjects as Daumier's. *The Absinthe Drinkers* sums up, as powerfully as any painting of the century, the futility of human life. Like so many of Degas's later pictures, this has a seemingly haphazard, "snapshotlike" composition, but one which is, in fact, carefully planned. Degas was a student of photography and liked to compose his pictures to give the impression that he had "observed his models through a keyhole." Although he did exhibit in the impressionist groups, his approach was even further from theirs than from Manet's. He always told people that "no art was ever less spontaneous than mine. What I do is the result of reflection and study of the great masters: of inspiration, spontaneity, temperament I know nothing."

Yet he freely experimented with the impressionistic treatment of figures in light, although in Degas's case it was more often theatrical footlighting than sunlight that interested him. He frequently worked in pastels rather than oil paint to aid him in his effects. (Pastel chalks had been used for sketches by masters since the seventeenth century, but it was not until the advent of Degas and his contemporaries that finished and full pastel works became widely admired.) The graceful steps of ballerinas on the stage, their diaphanous skirts a mere smudge of light, while their cohorts wait or relax in the wings, are given a light "impressionistic" treatment in pictures like *The Prima Ballerina* (Plate 93), although Degas's line is never lost. A similar treatment is given to the figures of the raucous singers of *The Café Concert: Les Ambassadeurs* (Plate 94), although the colors used and the rakishly sketched in audience suggest a different kind of entertainment.

Pierre Auguste Renoir (1841–1919), a tailor's son from Limoges, was apprenticed at the age of thirteen to a porcelain manufacturer,

91. *The Portrait of the Bellelli Family,* by Edgar Degas

92. *The Absinthe Drinkers,* by Edgar Degas

94. *The Cafe Concert: Les Ambassadeurs*, by Edgar Degas

93. *The Prima Ballerina,* by
Edgar Degas

and it was from porcelain decoration that he learned the value of clear, bright color. Some years later he applied himself to a serious course of art study in Paris, where his academic masters tried to discourage his love of vivid color. They must have partly succeeded, for when he was painting in the Forest of Fontainebleau in 1863, a man with a wooden leg appeared and, staring at his canvas, said, "Why the devil do you paint in such dark colors?" The man was Narciso Diaz de la Peña, one of the original Barbizon painters. For Renoir this meeting was almost as important as was the expedition with Boudin for Monet.

In fact, during a brief period when Renoir was studying at the studio of Charles Gabriel Gleyre, he met Monet. They became close friends and often painted together. But, whereas Monet, delighting in all of nature's aspects, painted crisply refreshing snow scenes, Renoir shuddered at what he described as "that malady of Nature" and was only inspired when the countryside blossomed beneath a warm sun. Nonetheless, he was deeply affected by Monet's experiments, and when they painted together, as they often did, their styles were very much alike.

But Renoir was not exclusively interested in landscape painting. He preferred figure painting, and his most important pictures are portraits, paintings of nudes, or scenes of crowds in restaurants or dance halls. Nor was Monet his chief influence. Renoir studied the old masters at the Louvre, and particularly admired Rubens and the Venetians such as Titian. In 1865 he met Courbet, who temporarily became his idol, but although Renoir tried to give his pictures a convincingly studied realism, they always have a bright, colorful grace and their mood is one of perpetual gaiety. Like Courbet and the realists, he portrayed the life of simple people, but his subjects are never grim or depressing.

Renoir's painting of *The Ball at the Moulin de la Galette* (Plate 95) is the high-water mark of his impressionist years. With thousands of tiny brushstrokes, Renoir has captured the effect of flickering light playing across a crowd of dancing couples, several of Renoir's friends among them.

Renoir was particularly famous for his nudes. His painting entitled *A Bather* (Plate 96) shows his debt to the old masters,

96. *A Bather,* **by Pierre Auguste Renoir**

and to Ruben's translucent blond flesh shades in particular. Renoir achieved his effects by means very different from those employed by Rubens. Whereas Rubens had used a technique of under painting on his canvases Renoir painted directly in little strokes of delicate hue. Of his portraits, his picture of Mme. Henriot (Plate 97) is among the most successful. Renoir was a great admirer of feminine beauty, and he ran to type, preferring to paint women with round faces and huge, gentle, dark eyes set far apart. His portraits of women were popular, and they brought him some measure of financial success.

The year of 1881 was a turning point in Renoir's life. In that year he painted *The Luncheon of the Boating Party* (Plate 98), a complicated composition showing the disarray of a carefree 159

95. *The Ball at the Moulin de la Galette,* by **Pierre Auguste Renoir**

party of leisurely lunchers who have just finished their meal on a terrace over the river (where their boat awaits them) and are lazing in the shade of a striped awning. This picture seems at first very much like Renoir's earlier work, but on closer examination it may be noticed that the outlines are more distinct, the figures more neatly executed and the colors more sharply contrasted. Renoir was finding the doctrines of impressionism too restricting.

In this picture Renoir has portrayed a group of his friends, and the young lady with pursed lips cuddling the lapdog on the left of the painting is Alice Charigat, whom he married later that year. He spent his honeymoon in Italy, where the antique paintings of Pompeii and Raphael's works in Rome led him to reconsider his aims; and indeed many of his later pictures reveal a startling change. For a while he abandoned the blurred tones of impressionism and defined his forms with a hard, delicate outline that is almost like Ingres's.

But in Renoir's last years he returned, of necessity, to his earlier style. From about 1888 on his health declined and he became increasingly crippled by rheumatism, so that he was eventually confined to a wheelchair and had to paint with a brush strapped to his wrist. His strokes became broad and rhythmical, and strong paintings like his *A Landscape with the Sea in the Distance* (Plate 99) prove that his spirit was unbowed. He spent his winters at Cagnes-sur-Mer in the south of France, and the hot, glowing colors of his canvases show his hunger for warmth and life to the very end.

Two more among the great masters of the impressionist movement remain to be considered. They are Camille Pissarro (1830–1903) and Alfred Sisley (1839–1899), who were friends, and whose works were often quite similar.

Camille Pissarro was not only one of the most important of the impressionist group, he was also a close link between his own generation and the younger artists who reacted vigorously against impressionism. Pissarro, who was of Spanish-Jewish descent, was born in St. Thomas in the West Indies. He started work as an assistant in his father's general store, but he spent his time drawing the scurrying sailors and dockers instead of checking the

97. *Portrait of Mme. Henriot,* **by Pierre Auguste Renoir**

98. *The Luncheon of the Boating Party,* by Pierre Auguste Renoir

99. *A Landscape with the Sea in the Distance,* by Pierre Auguste Renoir

cargoes being unloaded in the port. Finally his parents realized that it was useless to try to thwart their son's ambition to become a painter, and with their permission he set off for France, arriving in 1855. At that time the artistic circle in Paris was split into two factions: One supported the officially sponsored Exposition Universelle, which had just been honored by a visit from Queen Victoria; the other was attracted by the rebellious Courbet's realist exhibition. There was, however, one man following a middle course—Corot, who was modestly pursuing his own researches into nature.

Pissaro clearly realized that his chief interest was to be in landscape painting, for he plucked up his courage and called on Corot to ask for his advice. Corot received him kindly, and although he never gave regular instructions to students, he offered Pissarro guidance and criticism for many years; Monet was to remark how alike their paintings were.

Pissarro's *A Street in Louveciennes* (Plate 100), painted in 1872, shows how strong Corot's influence on him in fact was. He was also influenced by Courbet and took to using a palette knife for applying thick layers of paint to his canvases. Still, no dramatic change took place in Pissarro's art until some time after he had come back to France from England, where he had fled during the Franco-Prussian War. When in England, he displayed in his landscapes his careful study of Constable's sketches. Upon his return to France he settled in the village of Pontoise, where he began to develop fully his impressionist style, and he exhibited with the impressionists at the photographer Nadar's studio.

By 1877, when he painted *Spring at Pontoise* (Plate 101), Pissaro's impressionism had reached its most colorful and vivacious peak. But his canvases were crossed by strong vertical and horizontal lines—in this case the play of intersecting tree trunks and roofs. He feared the loss of clarity and strong composition (which he had learned from Corot) that results from a totally impressionistic treatment of any subject. By the 1880's he felt that impressionism was too "diffused," and he experimented with the other techniques that young painters were developing in opposition to it.

Like Monet, Pissarro suffered periods of terrible poverty, made worse by the fact that he had a large family. Yet he never settled for easy success, and always sought the style he felt would best fulfill his artistic demands. Despite his poverty, moreover, he always extended hospitality and encouragement to struggling young painters in whose talent he had confidence. Among the artists whom he befriended was the French-born Englishman, Alfred Sisley. Sisley had studied at Gleyre's studio, where he met Renoir, whom he joined on his expedition with Monet to paint in the Forest of Fontainebleau. Partly because he was a solitary investigator, he never played as important a role in French painting as did Monet, Renoir, and Pissarro. His painful shyness drove him to Louveciennes, where he made his significant discoveries alone. It is interesting to compare Sisley's *Snow at Louveciennes* (Plate 102) with Pissarro's painting of that village. Although Sisley's work is more freely impressionistic, the village must have given both painters the same feeling of placid human habitation, guarded in winter by the lofty skeletons of denuded trees. Sisley could capture many moods with his free, easy impressionism. In his picture *Flood at Port-Marly* (Plate 103), he has painted the precise hue that suggests the unnatural, chilly expanse of floodwater.

The latter part of the nineteenth century was the era of female emancipation. It is not surprising, then, that impressionism was the first important movement in the history of art to number women among its members. Both Berthe Morisot (1841–1895) and Mary Cassatt (1845–1926) were known for their paintings of mothers and children. Morisot, a student of Corot, was twice painted by Manet, who admired her extraordinary personality. Her painting *The Butterfly Hunt* (Plate 104) shows how well impressionism lent itself to the delicate, feminine handling of such an appealing subject. Mary Cassatt was an American, born in Pittsburgh, the sister of a president of the Pennsylvania Railroad. She came to Europe in 1875, spent some time in Spain, and then proceeded to Paris, where she won the friendship of Degas. Many

100. *A Street in Louveciennes,* **by Camille Pissarro**

101. *Spring at Pontoise,* **by Camille Pissarro**

102. *Snow at Louveciennes,* **by Alfred Sisley**

103. *Flood at Port-Marly,* by Alfred Sisley

172

of her earlier works show his influence, but later they quarreled, and after that Mary Cassatt's paintings, like *The Sisters* (Plate 105), while full of sweetness, betray a lack of the stern control of a master like Degas.

Paris was the unquestioned capital of the impressionist world. Strangely enough it was an American who undertook the difficult task of presenting impressionism to the British. James Abbott McNeill Whistler (1834–1903) was born in Lowell, Massachusetts. After a visit to Russia with his father at the age of seventeen, and an unsuccessful career as a West Point cadet and a naval draftsman, he set sail for England and in 1855 went to France, to study painting. He identified himself with the impressionists from the very beginning. Like Monet, Renoir, and Sisley, he too studied at the studio of Gleyre, a classicist of the Ingres school, who seems to have influenced his pupils chiefly by inspiring them to rebel. Whistler submitted a painting to the Salon, and when it was refused, he exhibited it at the Salon of the Rejected, or Salon des Refusés, where it scored a great success.

Although he was capable of using impressionist techniques, Whistler's main interest was not impressionism and the effects of light, but rather the patterns made by harmonious areas of color on his canvas. Like many of his contemporaries, he was fascinated by Japanese prints, which had originally come to Europe as the wrapping of merchandise, and which were soon appreciated for their own beauty. Some of Whistler's paintings, like *Fantasy in Blue and Green* (Plate 106), are fanciful interpretations of Japanese designs, impressionistically treated. His *Harmony in Gray and Green: Miss Cecily Alexander* (Plate 107), by contrast, does not so directly imitate the Japanese; it is a touching portrait of a young girl. But again Whistler has simplified everything down to what is indeed a "harmony" of gray and green patterns of color, and one feels that the careful placement of the hat, the black rosette at the girl's waist, the marguerites sprinkled beside her, and the butterflies above her head are perhaps more important to the artist than the character of the model herself. Whistler's "butterfly" signature is to be seen at the left of the picture.

104. *The Butterfly Hunt,*
by Berthe Morisot

105. *The Sisters,* **by Mary Cassatt**

Whistler had settled in London, where he remained for the better part of his working life. It is little wonder, with titles like *Harmony in Gray and Green,* and the concentration upon abstract patterns which such titles suggest, that he aroused the ire of John Ruskin, the champion of the pre-Raphaelites and their overdetailed, story-telling, and moralistic canvases. Moreover Ruskin and Whistler were probably the two grouchiest men of the period.

Whistler was a scrupulous dandy who got on so poorly with his fellow man that he even wrote an art study entitled *The Gentle Art of Making Enemies*. Ruskin was aging, well known for his ill humor, and on the brink of mental collapse in 1877, when Whistler exhibited a series of night scenes entitled *Nocturnes*. The *Nocturnes* were impressionists works, and Ruskin singled them out for special scorn.

Whistler priced his works at 200 guineas apiece. Ruskin's views on this were to the point; he wrote: "I have never expected to hear a coxcomb ask 200 guineas for flinging a pot of paint in the public's face." Whistler sued for libel, and the result was one

106. *Fantasy in Blue and Green,* **by James Abbott McNeill Whistler**

of the most heated lawsuits of the century. Impressionism itself was on trial, and it very nearly lost. Whistler won the case, but he was awarded all of one farthing in damages. Still, the defense had been so foolish that the impressionists were completely vindicated in the eyes of the public, and Ruskin, although he lost little, retired from the fray a broken man. During the trial, when asked how he dared to charge such a sum for what he admitted to be two days' work, Whistler had replied, "No, I ask it for the knowledge of a lifetime."

Ruskin felt that the ideas of impressionism were a threat to art as he knew it, and in that he was quite correct. The impressionists had, in their search for the realistic portrayal of light, broken the visual world down into patterns of color, so that it was seen as it had never been seen before. And it was destined never to look the same to artists again.

107. *Harmony in Gray and Green: Miss Cecily Alexander,* **by James Abbott McNeill Whistler**

The Postimpressionists and the End of the Nineteenth Century

THE IMPRESSIONISTS' canvases were delightfully decorative. Moreover, they had thrown off, once and for all, the chains which had held art to the minute depiction of reality. Still the technique of impressionism itself was, as we have seen, a limited one. Its splendid effects of light were often achieved at the sacrifice of solid form, composition, and emotional meaning. The next generation produced a group of brilliant painters who rebelled in one way or another against it. Their rebellion took various forms, resulting in the great movements of art in the twentieth century. It was not until 1911, after an impressive exhibition of the works of Cézanne, Vincent Van Gogh, and Paul Gauguin in London, that these painters, leaders of the rebellions, were dubbed "postimpressionists."

There were those among the younger painters who felt that if the ideas of impressionism could be more scientifically and systematically carried out, firmer boundaries and a more solid modeling of forms could be achieved. It was with this idea in mind that the eccentric painter, Georges Pierre Seurat (1859–1891), developed his theory of "pointillism," or "divisionism." In 1884, when Seurat was twenty-five, he exhibited his first major painting, the *Bathers at Asnières* (Plate 108). The past eight years had been a slow, deliberate, and secret preparation for that moment. Seurat had not shown at the École des Beaux-Arts, where his masters had considered him a serious but mediocre student. He had spent many hours in the Egyptian and Assyrian rooms of the Louvre, and he had modeled his drawings on Ingres.

Until 1883 Seurat painted very little. Drawing appeared to be his main concern, and he was never without a tiny sketching block, which he concealed in the palm of his hand. By this means he was able to draw undetected in cafés, at the circus, or on top of a bus on his way home from dining with his father—a

108. *Bathers at Asnières,* **by Georges Pierre Seurat**

secretive official with a strong streak of religious fanaticism—
from whom Seurat had inherited his retiring disposition. Inspired
by Millet, he worked with Conté crayon, a kind of hard, reddish
pastel, on a coarse watercolor paper, producing beautiful drawings in which he reduced the complex forms of trees, dresses, coal
barges, and so on to smooth abstract geometric shapes.

Seurat often worked in the neighborhood of Paris, at Asnières
and on the Isle of La Grande Jatte, on the Seine. He executed a
large number of sketches in preparation for his painting *Bathers
at Asnières,* and although he was not in touch with the impressionists, much of it is painted in a light impressionist style. But
despite its carefully achieved balmy, warm atmosphere, Seurat's
chief interest lay not in impressionistic effects of color, but in   181

the neat order of the smoothly outlined, rather geometric forms of the bathers, their paraphernalia, and even the trees and sails in the distance.

It was in 1884, when the picture was exhibited, that Seurat met Paul Signac (1863–1935), with whom he had much in common, and through him the impressionists. Under their influence he attempted a style employing broken strokes of color, but he adapted it to his own needs, developing the technique known as "divisionism." He had studied Chevreul's *Laws of Color Contrast* and other works, and he now replaced the flurries and flecks of impressionist handling with a calm, calculated system of dots of pure color set off by complementaries. This was a technique much like the careful method of "strippling" in color lithography, whereby a third color can be created by the combination of the dots of two other colors, as, for example, green resulting from microscopic dots of blue and yellow. Of course, Seurat's "dots" were not as small as those of lithography, and he used mixed colors as well as the primary red, yellow, and blue. The result was the clean, neatly outlined order that impressionism lacked, and yet Seurat did not lose its vibrant sunlight.

When Seurat's divisionist pictures were first exhibited to the public, they were derided as "flea paintings." Still Seurat kept to his course of developing what he called his "formula for optical painting." The Belgian poet Verhaeren, who knew Seurat well, said, "I think he had set himself to pull art clear of the hesitations of vagueness, indecision and imprecision." The next step for Seurat was to introduce movement into his work, and this he set about to do. He was fascinated with the circus, and many of his later sketches depict its thrills in an original way. His large canvas entitled *The Circus* (Plate 109) was left unfinished when Seurat died tragically of meningitis at the age of thirty-one. Although it is a totally pointillist picture, his style has been completely transformed. The scene, brought alive by flamelike figures, throbs with the swing of action and excitement: The ringmaster cracks his swirling whip, an acrobat somersaults, and the bareback rider's horse plunges across the sawdust.

182   It is impossible to predict what Seurat could eventually have

109. *The Circus*, by Georges Pierre Seurat

done, as he lived to paint only six important pictures. The seemingly foolproof nature of his theories attracted many other painters, including Paul Signac, who was Seurat's close friend and had worked along the same lines from the very beginning. Signac's painting of the shore at St. Tropez (Plate 110), done fourteen years after Seurat's death, shows less of an interest in geometric form, and this combined with his larger, more square 183

110. *St. Tropez,* by Paul Signac

stroke gives the picture the effect of a more free impressionist painting.

But, despite Seurat's numerous followers, pointillism proved eventually to be only an interesting experiment. No final "formula for optical painting" was to be found, and other figures among the "postimpressionists" affected the progress of art more deeply. Of these, three stand out, the three who were exhibited together in London in 1911: Paul Cézanne, Vincent Van Gogh, and Paul Gauguin.

Cézanne (1839–1906) was of the same generation as the impressionists. When he first arrived in Paris in 1861, his sensitivity earned him the nickname of "L'Ecorché," likening him to an artist's anatomical figure showing muscles, and therefore without a skin. He spent the next decade living partly in Paris and partly in his birthplace, Aix-en-Provence, in the south of France, painting turbulent scenes inspired by the Italian Renaissance masters, Veronese, Giorgione, and others, in a somewhat heavily executed impressionist manner. Two friendships supported him, that of his former schoolmate, the novelist Émile Zola, and that of Camille Pissarro, whom he met in 1863. Cézanne attended the impressionists' gatherings at the Café Guerbois, but would often sit morosely in a corner. He distrusted theorizing, and as an old man he would cut short queries on aesthetic theory by flying into a rage, but in 1872 Pissarro invited him to join him at Pontoise, and Cézanne never ceased to be grateful to him for thus introducing him to the close study of nature. They set up their easels side by side, and, inspired by Pissarro, Cézanne began to notice the "atmospheric" effect of light. Paintings like *The House of the Hanged Man at Auvers-sur-Oise* (Plate 111) were the result. Although he exhibited with them in 1874, Cézanne was not a success as an impressionist. He never mastered the light, easy impressionist touch and always had to search slowly for the exact colors of the scene before he added layer upon layer of heavy paint, so that the results of his attempts at imitation were somewhat clumsy.

Cézanne spent the greater part of his time, from 1884 on, in Aix-en-Provence, eventually settling there for good. He had a comfortable private income, and without the need to please patrons, he set about developing the style for which he later became famous. Two apparently contradictory statements sum up his aims. He said that he wanted "to make of impressionism something solid and durable, like the art of the museums," and at the same time he wanted to "do Poussin [the great French classical landscape painter of the seventeenth century] over from nature." What he meant, in effect, was that he wanted to introduce the light and the atmospheric effects of the impressionists to the solid, orderly compositions of the classicists. In a way, his basic objective was the same as Seurat's, but he set about achieving it in a very different way.

111. The House of the Hanged Man at Auvers-sur-Oise, by Paul Cézanne

112. *Mont Sainte-Victoire,* **by Paul Cézanne**

He painted canvas after canvas of the scenery of his native Provence—the olive groves, the vineyards and orchards giving way to the harsh dusty uplands that ascend to the bare summit of Mont Sainte-Victoire, (Plate 112). In a combination of sensitive line and delicate, square or "hatched" brushstrokes, he minutely depicted each successive plane of the view in front of him. Unlike the impressionists, he wanted to use color to model what he felt to be the underlying and permanent form of the object he was looking at. The exact shape and shade of every inch of even the most far-distant mountain seems to have been carefully considered. The result is that although Cézanne's perspective is technically far from perfect (and in his later works he overthrew

188

the rules of perspective altogether), he achieves the most extra-ordinary effect of a third dimension. In the *Mont Sainte-Victoire* reproduced here, one literally feels oneself looking down into the distance at the aquaduct running at the foot of the mountain.

With time Cézanne began to rely more and more upon water-color. He applied tints of apricot, rose, lavender, emerald, or ultramarine blue, in light washes to the shadows, leaving the rest of the picture untouched. So exact was their placing, however, that the whole of a complex form was instantly visible. These experiments enabled him to apply his oil paint in the translucent, unhesitating touches that made his effects of warm atmosphere and distance possible.

Cezanne said that "all forms in nature are modeled upon the cone, the sphere and the cylinder," and he concentrated with intensity on the exact pattern of lines that create the shape of things and gives them a sense of volume, sometimes to the point of disregarding all else. He was by no means entirely a landscape artist, and his painting of the cardplayers whom he observed in the local café is one of his best-known works (Plate 113). Their deep thought is as evident as that of Daumier's chess players, and so is their solidity, their weight, as they lean on the table. But in a way, the picture is also a study executed in right angles. The design created by the bounding lines of Cézanne's shapes had be-come all-important.

This is true, too, of the many still lifes Cézanne painted in his later years. In his picture entitled *The Blue Vase* (Plate 114), considerations of perspective are thrown to the winds. He has been careful about the shapes of the apples, the shapes of the leaves and flowers, but the dish does not really stand behind the vase.

Cézanne did not receive a great deal of recognition in his life-time. He was particularly bitter when his old friend, Zola, car-icatured him as an unsuccessful painter in one of his novels. Cezanne was cut to the quick and they quarreled, but when he heard the news of Zola's death sixteen years later, he is said to have burst into tears.

Zola had often come to young Cézanne's aid when his father, 189

113. *The Cardplayers,* **by Paul Cézanne**

a well-to-do banker, had kept him short of money. At last, in 1885, Cézanne had placated his father by marrying, and the following year the older Cézanne had died, leaving his son a considerable fortune. Still, despite his comfort, Cézanne's life had been a disappointment. He had been constantly rejected in his youth and middle years, and although he finally won the admira-

114. *The Blue Vase*, **by Paul Cézanne**

tion of artistic circles in his old age, it came too late. He said
to his young friend, Vollard, "I have made some progress. Why so
late, and with such difficulty? Is art indeed a priesthood which
demands the pure in heart, completely dedicated to it?"

By the time Cezanne died in 1906 he had provided the inspiration for the cubists, led by Braque and Picasso, who broke all

visible reality down into compositions of shifting planes. The cubists agreed with the sentiment he expressed in one of his few confident remarks: "There is only one living painter, myself."

Unsuccessful though Cézanne may have felt his life to have been, it was not pure tragedy like Van Gogh's. For Van Gogh, what impressionism lacked was strong emotional power and appeal to the deeper sentiments. To him the works of the impressionists were pretty decorations, but they did nothing to evoke the sorrow of the human soul. An expressionist artist is primarily one who has strong opinions or emotions which he seeks to impress upon the spectator, and the word "expressionist" was coined to describe Van Gogh.

The son of a Dutch Calvinist pastor, Vincent Van Gogh (1853–1890) tried his hand at several professions before devoting himself solely to his career as an artist, although painting was always uppermost in his mind. Fortunately he corresponded continually with his younger brother Theo, to whom he clearly described what he sought to express and the means he used to translate these ideas into pictorial form. Often he prefaced these descriptions with the words "I want to express . . . ," pathetically adding sometimes, "If people don't understand, I don't care." It was pathetic because he cared enormously, and when the public rejected his art, he felt that they had rejected him as a person.

Human relations were especially dear to him, but they invariably ended in failure. He longed passionately for a wife and family, yet women brought him nothing but misery. His friendships with his fellow artists were equally difficult. His love for humanity led him to try a religious vocation in the mining district of the Borinage, but his zeal was excessive. Moreover, his unkempt appearance and abject poverty alarmed the villagers, who expected a minister to live in a tidy house and wear clean linen. After a mining explosion his devotion in nursing the wounded and comforting the bereaved caused them to change their opinions, but by then it was too late; his spirit was broken.

Upon giving up his religious calling, Van Gogh wrote his brother a letter which explains something of his tortured nature:

You must not think that I disavow things; I am rather faithful in my unfaithfulness, and though changed, I am the same, and my only anxiety is: how can I be of use in the world, cannot I serve some purpose and be of any good.

Well, what shall I say: our inward thoughts, do they ever show outwardly? There may be a great fire in our soul and no one ever comes to warm himself at it, and the passers-by see only a little bit of smoke coming through the chimney and pass on their way. Now look here, what must be done? Must one tend that inward fire, have salt in oneself, wait patiently, yet with how much impatience for the hour when somebody will come and sit down near it—to stay there maybe.

A caged bird in spring knows quite well that he might serve to some end; he feels quite well that there is something for him to do, but he cannot do it. What is it? He does not remember quite well. Then he has some vague ideas and says to himself "The others make their nests and lay their eggs and bring up their little ones." And then he knocks his head against the bars of the cage. But the cage stands there and the bird is maddened by anguish.

And men are often prevented by circumstances from doing things, a prisoner in I do not know what horrible, horrible, most horrible cage. There is also, I know it, the deliverance, the tardy deliverance. A just or unjustly ruined reputation, poverty, fatal circumstances, adversity, that's what makes men prisoners.

One cannot always tell what it is that keeps us shut in, confines us, seems to bury us, but, however, one feels certain barriers, certain gates, certain walls. Is all this imagination, fantasy? I do not think so. And then one asks: "My God! Is it for long, is it forever, is it for eternity?" Do you know what frees one from this captivity? It is every deep serious affection. Being friends, being brothers, love, that is what opens the prison by supreme power, by some magic force.

Van Gogh found solace for this bitter anguish in drawing, and it was now, in 1880, at the age of twenty-seven, that he discovered his vocation as an artist. He would use the brush to communicate the full depth of his feelings.

He entered the studio of Anton Mauve, a cousin and a success- 193 ful artist, in The Hague, but after two years he returned to his father's parsonage at Nuenen. Inevitably, when he returned home, his family felt as strongly about his uncouth ways as had his parish. "There is a similar reluctance to have me at home as there would be to have a big clumsy dog in the house," he wrote. "He comes into the rooms with wet paws—and in any case, he is so shaggy. He gets in everybody's way. And he barks so loudly. In short, he is a dirty animal." The "dirty animal," as he called himself, was convinced that art must rest on moral values.

Degas's seamstresses at work or his exhausted dancers, Renoir's boaters in their shirt sleeves, all were translated by these painters into a lovely pattern of colors. With the exception of *The Absinthe Drinkers* and a few other paintings, there is little humanity in the work of the impressionists, let alone human suffering. The impressionists were apparently untroubled by the social matters that interested Courbet and Daumier. Manet was a liberal-minded democrat, Degas a reactionary royalist, Pissarro a socialist, yet they were all friends, and united in their interest in light and color. Now Van Gogh, a fervent admirer of Millet, wanted to present scenes of social comment, to portray poverty as he knew it to be. He asked Theo to send him engravings of pictures depicting soup kitchens and similar scenes of deprivation.

All his ambitions during this period were enshrined in his painting *The Potato Eaters* (Plate 115). He admired Rembrandt's portraits of the poor, and this may account for the darkness of his palette. His coarse, blunt brushstrokes were wonderfully suited to the peasants' heavy, dulled expressions and clumsy gestures. The thin light points up their gnarled fingers and snubbed features. Van Gogh said, "I have tried to make it clear how these people, eating their potatoes under the lamplight, have dug the earth with those very hands which they put in the dish. . . ."

Theo was by now successfully settled in Paris and working for an art dealer. Vincent was lured by his descriptions of impressionist paintings and arrived in Paris suddenly in 1886. Through Theo he met Seurat, Pissarro, Gauguin, and Henri de Toulouse-Lautrec (1864–1901). Influenced by the ideas of these men, he took to

lightening his palette and painting in a fluent impressionistic style

115. *The Potato Eaters,* by Vincent Van Gogh

—but his was a new impressionist technique of agitated and swirling or sharp and staccato brushstrokes, full of his own torment, so that the surfaces of his canvases resembled "fields of stubble."

For his *Self-Portrait* painted in 1887, he adopted Seurat's divisionist technique and theories of color. The whole is executed in short, equal brushstrokes in the constrasting shades of orange and blue. But nothing could be further from Seurat's calmly calculated compositions. The portrait is a work of anguished, nervous sensitivity, and perfectly true to the character of the artist. The following is an eyewitness description of Van Gogh at the time:

> I can affirm that . . . Van Gogh was a weedy little man with pinched features, red hair and beard and a light blue eye. He had an extraordinary way of pouring out sentences in Dutch, English, and French, then glancing back over his shoulder and hissing through his teeth. In fact, when thus excited he looked more than a little mad: at other times he was apt to be morose as if suspicious. To tell the truth, I fancy that the French were civil to him largely because his brother Theodore was employed by Goupil and Company and so bought pictures.

Vincent longed for the south, and in February 1888, after two years in Paris, he departed, with the aid of his brother, for Arles in Provence. When the spring came, the light color and rampant bloom on the gnarled fruit trees intoxicated him, and he painted in frenzied excitement. He was attracted by the warmth and vitality of the landscape and poured out all his love and energy in trying to represent it. He painted several portraits of the few local inhabitants with whom he had become friendly, but for him the south was really represented by the dark twisted and tortured cypress trees. When he painted sunflowers (Plate 116) he brilliantly adapted his strokes to the textures of the various parts of the flowers, yet their twisted and shriveled petals make them appear almost more frightening than beautiful.

And yet, despite the artistic success of his stay in the south, despair followed: Theo failed to sell his brother's pictures in Paris, and Vincent became increasingly lonely. Then briefly his

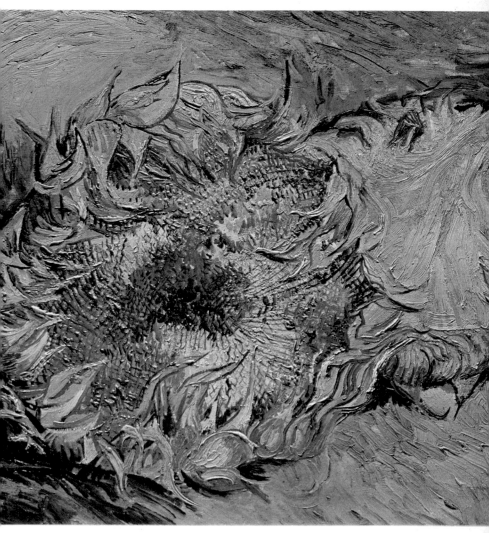

116. *Sunflowers,* **by Vincent Van Gogh**

spirits rose. He moved into his "Yellow House," which he dreamed of as the "House of Friends," a refuge for painters. The first visitor was Gauguin, and many of Van Gogh's pictures of this time resemble in their broad, decorative, colored shapes, 197

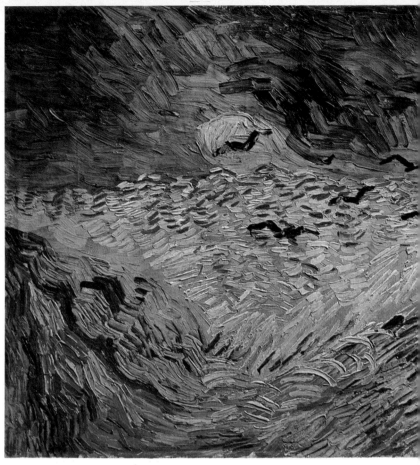

117. *Cornfield with Crows,* **by Vincent Van Gogh**

the paintings of Gauguin. But the friendship of the two artists was doomed. Gauguin was competent, ruthless, and egotistical. One night they quarreled; Vincent attacked him with a knife, and then cut off his own ear in remorse. He had gone mad. Gauguin fled, the neighbors were terrified, and Vincent was admitted to a hospital.

From now on Van Gogh's inner turmoil was reflected in his paintings, and he drove his brush across his pictures in thick, rhythmical strokes and even squeezed the paint directly from the tube in whorls onto the canvas. In several of his pictures of this period the forms were so exaggerated that the whole world seemed

to be erupting. As his attacks of madness increased in frequency
and violence, he was taken to the home of a doctor. His last paintings were of vast empty cornfields menaced by black crows
wheeling overhead (see Plate 117). On July 27, 1890, he borrowed
a gun to shoot the birds. His misery was absolute, he turned the
shotgun on himself. As he had said in a letter so many years before, ". . . it might happen that the dog goes mad one day and
bites someone, and then the gamekeeper would have to be called
in to shoot him dead. All right! . . ."

If Cézanne distorted the visual world to get at its inner, more
permanent form, Van Gogh distorted it to give a sense of passion- 199

ate emotion. Expressionism was, like cubism, a cornerstone of twentieth-century art. All that was needed to complete the foundation for art today was Gauguin's haunting symbolism.

In January of 1883, Paul Gauguin (1848–1903), a Frenchman of part-Peruvian descent, resigned from the stockbrokerage firm of Bertin. He was thirty-four years old and convinced that his destiny was to become a painter. Leaving the brokerage firm had been a radical step. He was rich, married to Mette Gad, the daughter of a Danish poet, and the father of a large family. He had been painting for the last ten years, but only in his spare time. From 1880 on, he had exhibited with the impressionists, whose style he had adopted, but it was unkindly rumored that they tolerated his early efforts because they could not offend such a generous patron, for Gauguin had purchased a splendid collection of impressionist pictures.

By 1885, his fortunes had declined catastrophically, and from then until his death he led the life of a vagabond. That winter he was forced to take up employment as a billposter; he also left his wife. But in the next years matters improved artistically, if not materially. He went to Brittany, and there, staying at the modest Pension Gloanec in Pont-Aven, he met the painter Émile Bernard (1868–1941), with whom he was later to develop a close but stormy relationship. Bernard was not as gifted as Gauguin, but he had a sharp intelligence and was clever at theorizing. His style was bold, sharply outlined, and somewhat like Cézanne's. Gauguin's earlier pictures had been curiously dull, but now in Brittany he began to brighten his color and clarify his shapes. Of Brittany he said, "I find wildness and primitiveness there. When my wooden shoes ring on the granite, I hear the muffled, dull and powerful tone which I try to achieve in painting." In December of 1886 he met Van Gogh in Paris. But his first true artistic revelation came the following year, in 1887, when his lack of money induced him to go to Panama and work as a digger on the canal. From there he went on to Martinique, where he was dazzled by the colorful landscape and the native population.

On his return from Martinique Gauguin stayed once more at 200 Pont-Aven, where Émile Bernard was installed, and was pursuing his theory of what he called "synthetism," and becoming increasingly inspired by medieval art. Both artists were struck by the vitality of the Breton calvaries—simple folk-art carvings of Christ on the Cross—which they came across in the local country lanes. They also examined the strongly primitive shapes and vividly contrasted colors of medieval stained-glass windows. Gauguin immediately tried to translate what he saw into contemporary scenes, thus, his local peasants in traditional costume kneel before a wayside crucifix that becomes, in his *Yellow Christ* (Plate 118), a true Christ on the Cross. In this scene of the spiritual

118. *Yellow Christ*, by Paul Gauguin

imagination, Gauguin encloses his figures in hard, clear outline, placing them against a landscape of flat yellow.

A new style was clearly taking shape. Unnoticed by most Parisians, an exhibition was held in the Café Volpini in 1889 of the works of a new group calling themselves "synthetist-symbolists," which was headed by Gauguin. The synthetist-symbolists were opposed to all forms of naturalism and realism. The symbolists were concerned with creating images from the imagination that would "symbolize" certain states of feelings, such as love, hope, or fear, or the exaltation inspired by music or poetry; they sought "to clothe the idea in sensible form," as they put it. Synthetism was the technique in which these "symbolic" pictures were to be painted. Bernard lectured on the doctrine, but it was best summed up by the young painter Maurice Denis (1870–1943) when he described his introduction to the works of Gauguin:

> It was on our reassembling in 1888 that the name of Gauguin was revealed to us by Sérusier [Paul Sérusier, 1863–1927], who had just returned from Pont-Aven and who allowed us to see, not without a show of mystery, the lid of a cigar box, on which we could make out a shapeless landscape synthetically designed in violet, vermillion, Veronese green and other unmixed colors, just as they are pressed out of a tube, almost without white in them. "How does that tree appear to you?" Gauguin had asked —"Very green?—Well then use green—the finest green on your palette—and that shadow is rather blue? Do not be afraid to paint it as blue as possible . . ." Thus was presented to us for the first time the fruitful conception of the plane surface covered with colors put together in a certain order . . . we learned that every work of art is a transposition caricature, the passionate equivalent of sensation which has been experienced. . . .Gauguin freed us from all restraints which the idea of copying placed on our painters' instincts. . . . Henceforth we aspired to express our own personality. . . . If it was permissible to use vermillion in painting a tree which seemed to us at that moment reddish, . . . why not stress, even to the point of deformation, the curve of a beautiful shoulder, exaggerate the pearly whiteness of a carnation, stiffen the symmetry of boughs unmoved by a breath of air?

The following year Gauguin made the acquaintance of a group of writers headed by the poets Stéphane Mallarmé and Charles Morice, whose experiments and ideas represented a development of symbolism in literature similar to that which was taking place in painting at Pont-Aven. Amid this general revolt against realism, the writer Péladan attempted to create a cult of magical religious thought, and the novelist Huysmans made Des Esseintes, the hero of his *Against the Grain,* an eccentric who never saw the light of day and could enjoy only artificial pleasures. Morice described the somewhat startling appearance of Gauguin when he first met him:

> A broad face, massive and bony, a narrow forehead, a nose neither curved nor arched, but as if broken, a thin-lipped mouth without any inflection, heavy eyelids lifting sluggishly over somewhat protuberant eyeballs whose bluish pupils rotated in their orbits to glance to left or right while his head and bust made almost no effort to turn. There was little charm about this stranger; yet he attracted one by his very personal expression, a mixture of haughty nobility, obviously innate, and of simplicity. . . .

Gauguin took to joining the meetings of these men at the Café Voltaire every Monday evening and quickly formed a wide circle of friends.

But despite the stimulation of their company, he was beginning to find European civilization increasingly sickening and constricting; moreover, he needed to retreat to a remote spot where he could live more cheaply. By April, 1891, his disillusionment with Europe had become complete and after the symbolists had given him a farewell banquet at the Café Voltaire, he set sail for Tahiti. He said prophetically, "I want to forget all the evils of the past and to die down there unknown by those here, free to paint without any glory at all for the others. . . . A terrible ordeal is in store in Europe for the coming generation: the Kingdom of Gold. Everything is rotten, men as well as the arts."

Gauguin remained in Tahiti until the end of his life, returning to France only briefly to settle his affairs. But his poverty made the problems of his life immense, even there. His own irritability, combined with his suspicion of the local officials, mostly bumbling bureaucrats who no doubt found him a thorn in their side, caused him a great deal of trouble. Still, despite adversity, he painted the most brilliant of his canvases, and it was his poverty and his lack of artistic materials that led him to experiment with wood carving, and, when he had studied the local primitive art, with woodcuts.

Gauguin was deeply interested in the local legends and beliefs of the natives. These tales enriched the symbolism of his pictures, and he moved freely between the world of observed appearances and the realm of magical fantasy. Above all the mysterious lethargy of the natives and their graceful, solid forms suited his temperament. Meanwhile his technique became stronger. He gave up the flat, hard-edged shapes of his Brittany pictures in favor of the more delicately modeled forms of works such as his *Tahitian Girls Bearing Mango Blossoms* (Plate 119). And he reduced his background space to shallow planes of emerald, lavender, sapphire, jade, carmine, and saffron.

In his painting entitled simply *Siesta, Tahiti* (Plate 120), he has dispensed altogether with the conventional skyline, adopting instead a high viewpoint, so that he can look down on the scene, and his attention is focused on the flat pattern formed by the girls' bodies in their gaily-colored costumes.

Gauguin's greatest masterpiece is one of the last of his Tahitian paintings, intriguingly entitled *Whence Do We Come? What Are We? Whither Are We Going?* (Plate 121). It was painted under the most tragic circumstances, which he described in a letter to a close friend:

> As soon as the mail arrived, having received nothing from Chaudet, my health all at once almost recovered, that is to say with no further chance of dying a natural death, I wanted to kill myself. I went off to hide in the mountains, where my corpse would have been devoured by the ants. I had no revolver, but I had some arsenic, treasured up during my attack of eczema; I don't know whether the dose was too strong or

119. *Tahitian Girls Bearing Mango Blossoms*, by Paul Gauguin

120. *Siesta, Tahiti,* **by Paul Gauguin**

whether the vomiting canceled the effect of the poison by throwing it up. Anyhow, after a night of terrible suffering, I went home . . . . This month I received 700 fr. from Chaudet and 150 fr. from Mauffra: with that I shall pay the most relentless of my creditors and go on yet again, living as before, in poverty and disgrace until May, when the bank will distrain on me and sell for a song what little I possess, my pictures among the rest. Well, when that time comes we'll see how to try again in some way. I may say that my mind was definitely made up for the month of December. So before dying I wanted to paint a large picture I had in my head, and right through the month I worked day and night in an extraordinary fever. It was all done without a model, dashed off, on a coarse knotty piece of sacking, so it looks terribly rough . . . . I put in it all my energy, a passion so dolorous, amid circumstances so terrible, and so clear was my vision that the haste of the execution is lost and life surges up. It does not stink of models, or technique, or of pretended rules, of which I have always fought shy, though sometimes with fear. It is a canvas 4 meters 50 long and 1 meter 70 high. The two upper corners are chrome yellow, with an inscription on the left and my name on the right, like a fresco whose corners are spoiled with age and which is appliquéd upon a golden wall. To the right at the lower end a sleeping child and three crouching women. Two figures dressed in purple confide their thoughts to one another. An enormous crouching figure, out of all proportion and intentionally so, raises its arms and stares in astonishment at these two, who dare to think of their destiny; a figure in the center is picking fruit; two cats near a child; a white goat; an idol, its arms mysteriously raised in a sort of rhythm seems to indicate the Beyond. Then, lastly, an old woman nearing death appears to accept everything . . . . She completed the story . . . . It is all on the bank of a river in the woods. In the background the ocean, then the mountains of a neighboring island. Despite changes of tone the coloring of the landscape is constant—either blue or Veronese green. Where does the execution of a painting commence, and where does it end? At that moment when the most intense emotions are in fusion in the depths of one's being, when they burst forth like lava from a volcano . . . ? The work is created suddenly, brutally if you like, and is not its appearance great, almost superhuman?

This was the very essence of symbolism. The deep philosophic inquiry of such a work put Gauguin at the opposite pole from the impressionists. In 1898 Maurice Denis wrote to ask him if he would exhibit with the symbolists and the pointillists the

121. *Whence Do We Come? What Are We? Whither Are We Going?* by Paul Gauguin

following year. Gauguin turned the invitation down, testily declaring that he would not exhibit with artists who hailed him as a follower instead of recognizing him as their leader. But his health was failing, and living now in the Marquesas Islands he was forced to work in a Government office at six francs a day to pay off his taxes. He died on May 9, 1903, and was buried in the local mission cemetery of one of the islands.

Apart from the giants of the period, there were some most extraordinary painters whose talents flowered at the end of the century; among these, Henri Rousseau (1844–1910), called *Le Douanier* ("The Customs Official") because he spent his life in that capacity, and the aristocrat Henri de Toulouse-Lautrec (1864–1901) must be mentioned.

Rousseau was surely one of the strangest artists of any century. Although Gauguin aimed at a style that was inspired by the primitive, Rousseau was a true "primitive" in that he was entirely untaught. Curiously enough, the result of his self-education was, with regard to technique, a style much like that of the self-taught primitive painters of the American colonies. Rousseau's subject matter, however, was not the simple family scenes of the early Americans, but weird visions from his own imagination.

Until recently it was thought that Rousseau had served in the army in Mexico, but it is now known that the wild beasts and exotic jungles that figure so prominently in his imaginative fantasies were derived entirely from long hours spent in the zoo and the botanic gardens of Paris. There he brought a painstakingly observant eye to the study of the most minute details of leaf structure or the anatomy of a particular animal, and later he would assemble these things one by one in haunting paintings like *The Snake Charmer*, in which by the twilight of a pale moon, a mysterious and exotic creature pipes in a forest of giant plants, inhabited by huge serpents.

In his painting entitled *War* (Plate 122), Rousseau has, out of his very innocence, created a scene of remarkable power which now ranks as one of the great visionary paintings of the nineteenth century. War is represented as a hideous, witchlike figure galloping on a bridling steed over the multilated bodies of the dead and wounded, who are being devoured by vultures. The stark tree trunks, the flying legs and tail of the horse, the vultures' wings all suggest a painful terror.

At the age of sixteen, while convalescing in a hotel in Nice from the two accidents which were to leave him a cripple for life, Henri de Toulouse-Lautrec wrote, for the amusement of his cousin, the following description of a ball:

I went to the gallery. The musicians were there, a piano (belonging to the hotel), a cello and a violin. Then the male guests arrived. There were two officers, one of whom was here two years ago. *Dzin, boum, boum,* the ball began, with four young ladies to dance. People were beginning to mutter that it wasn't worth it (two young English ladies staying at the hotel, the most enthusiastic dancers, were ill) when a flock of innocent beauties arrived on the scene, we may mention in passing Mlle. Lecouteur (who has completed her 35th year), Mlle. Armiteze (a female chimpanzee, sister of the clergyman, 50 years in the fog) and Mlle. Ludlow (who laughs like a hen and midway between the two). The first two had opened their hearts and were revealing a fine set of violin strings *Dzin, boum, boum . . .* it filled up with two or three Misses and two young widows in black satin (where will mourning perch next!) *Dzin, boum, boum,* (now that is for me), Mme. V., in black velvet (what d'you think of that?), and M. Fitssoff running to a corner near the buffet with the two Captains, Morgan and Campbell. I was congratulating myself on my position when Attchoo!!! AAAAt!!! choo!!! Everyone began to sneeze. The dancing young ladies struggled desperately not to sneeze; their partners likewise; one man simply abandoned his partner and went off to a corner for a quarter of an hour. Old Captain Campbell was convinced he had a bad cold, so was M. Levy. Captain Morgan was just assuring us that he wasn't in the least under the general influence, when . . . .

Despite his disability, Lautrec retained his gaiety, and his lively powers of observation, throughout his short life. But for the double disaster that crippled both his legs he might never have

122. *War,* **by Henri Rousseau**

become a painter. Originally he was destined to live the life of
a country gentleman, as was fitting for a son of Comte Alphonse
de Toulouse-Lautrec. At first his parents, whose amateur interest
in the arts was confined to the sporting print, encouraged him to
amuse himself by drawing. Later he went to Paris and studied
at Cormon's academy, run by Fernard Piestre, a professor at the
École des Beaux Arts. There Lautrec acquired a conventional

Henri Rousseau

discipline and met Émile Bernard and later Van Gogh, whose art he was to defend in Brussels by challenging a detractor to a duel.

Because of his accident his legs never grew and he had the physical proportions of a dwarf. But he was witty and extremely popular with people of all classes, moving easily from Parisian society, which he rarely depicted, to the company of dancers and the demimonde of Montmartre. Perhaps because of what he con-

213

sidered to be his own ugliness, he had a great sympathy, as did Van Gogh, for the poor, especially pathetic dance-hall and circus performers. He was an admirer of Degas's dance-hall pictures, and he learned much of his technique and composition from a close study of Degas's works.

More than any other artist, Lautrec caught the spirit of the "Gay Paris" of the 1890's. His line was as accurate and unerring as Daumier's in vivacious pictures like his sketch of Jane Avril, the skinny, redheaded English dancer who fascinated him at the Moulin Rouge a dance hall which was made eternally famous by his brilliant drawings and paintings, not only of its performers, but also of its gay, bored, and worldly-wise clientele (Plate 123). Moreover, Lautrec had what Daumier lacked—a brilliant and original sense of color. He would, for example, use a vivid blue to shadow a face haggard and overpowdered. As at the age of sixteen, he saw everything.

One of the most important facets of Lautrec's art was the skill with which he designed posters. Here everything had to be reduced to bold linear pattern filled in with flat areas of color. Among the enthusiastic admirers of Lautrec's posters was the cabaret owner and entertainer, Aristide Bruant, who insisted on displaying them despite the protests occasionally raised by the singers themselves: "For the love of heaven, do not make me quite so ugly," implored Yvette Guilbert. Lautrec was adept at seizing upon the essentials of each act, and in the posters May Milton, the original "Little Girl," and May Belfort, of "Daddy wouldn't buy me a bow-wow" fame, are immortalized forever. But he could also evoke the elevated excitement of classical drama, and one of his most inspired posters announced Racine's *Phèdre* with Sarah Bernhardt, then in her heyday.

In 1899, because of his excessive drinking, Lautrec was confined in a sanatorium at Neuilly. On his release he humorously sent his friends an invitation to a milk party to celebrate, but his cure was short-lived, for he went back to drink. He was an indefatigable worker, and inevitably his physique collapsed under the strain. Two years later he was dead.

214   The easy, flowing lines and fastidious decorative details of Lau-

124. A Poster Announcing the Appearance of Jane Avril at the Jardin de Paris, by Henri de Toulouse-Lautrec

trec's posters—even two or three hairs on the musician's finger contribute vitally to the design of the Jane Avril poster (Plate 124) —remind us how close Lautrec was to the Art Nouveau movement. In 1895 he had paid his first visit to London, where he met Aubrey Vincent Beardsley and Oscar Wilde.

"Art Nouveau," which means simply "New Art," was a style that principally affected the decorative arts, book illustration, and typography, and it had clearly defined characteristics. It was 215

123. *The Moulin Rouge,* by Henri de Toulouse-Lautrec

distinguished above all by a sinuous, ever-flowing line which can be compared to the intertwining tendrils of the morning-glory, tresses blown in the wind, and eddying water. Its complicated designs closely resembled those of ancient Celtic art, which had just been rediscovered.

Art Nouveau designers were occupied largely with the minor arts. They produced furniture, tapestries, wallpapers, book-bindings, and glassware—for example, the glass vases (Plate 125) made by Louis Tiffany in America. Figures like that of Spring in

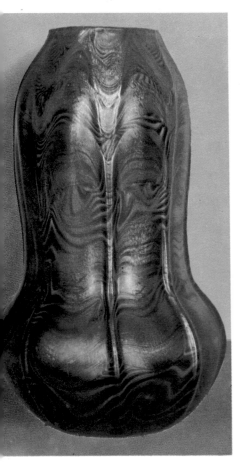

125. Glass vases, by Louis C. Tiffany

217

Eugène Grasset's stained-glass window (Plate 126) showed that the artistic ancestry of Art Nouveau was to be found in the work of the pre-Raphaelites. A great many decorative objects were created, like Frans Hoosman's candlestick (Plate 127), which consists of an ivory figure entwined in the stem and leaves of a typical languorously drooping plant, or René Lalique's decorated plate (Plate 128). Primarily Art Nouveau was a style of interior decoration. Rooms were no longer to be filled with miscellaneous bric-a-brac, objects variously collected and randomly exhibited—the full yet scrappy interior of the Victorian drawing room was now passé. The Art Nouveau designers threw out all this variegated junk, let in more light, and sought to make everything in the room, in the whole house, conform to one ruling standard of taste (Plate 129). A typical figure of the movement was Henry van de Velde. He started off as a fairly talented painter in a postimpressionist style, but gave this up for architecture and design, feeling that it was in these areas that he could most usefully combat the ugliness he found so appalling in the world around him. In this he was clearly influenced by the ideas of Ruskin, which prevailed throughout the Art Nouveau period. He also showed the fastidiousness mentioned above. Everything had to be correct, down to the last detail: He designed dresses for his wife to match the room she would be in, and felt that tomatoes, being red, ought to be served on green plates.

Art Nouveau lent itself well to book illustration, because of its decorative qualities. For instance, Caldecott's and Kate Greenaway's children's books were illustrated in a charming Art Nouveau style, and were popular in France as well as England. It is not surprising, then, that although Art Nouveau influenced several great painters, Lautrec, Gauguin, and other symbolists among them, the one great artist which it produced was an illustrator. Aubrey Beardsley's short career (1872–1898) flavored the whole of the 1890's in England.

Beardley's genius was discovered early, which was fortunate, as he lived only to the age of twenty-five. In the brief period of his creative life he made numerous illustrations—fascinating patterns in stark black and white areas, delineated by an endless

218

126. *Spring*, stained-glass window, by Eugène Grasset

127. Candlestick: the support in silver and the figure in ivory,
     by Frans Hoosmans
128. Decorated plate, by René Lalique

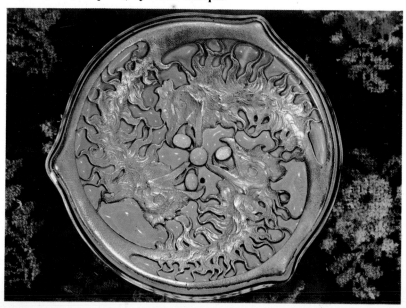

129. Corner of a drawing room, with wool tapestry

decorative line. But Beardsley's were more than mere illustrations. In their beautiful, fairy tale-like way they actually caricatured the society Beardsley had come to despise, and people were horrified to find themselves seeing "Beardsley faces" in the crowd. It is said that he managed to depict with exquisite beauty that which had lost its beauty, and at the same time to suggest evil.

Beardsley himself was the most extraordinary of figures, with, as a friend put it, "his butterfly ties, his too-smart clothes with their hard, padded shoulders; his face, as Oscar [Wilde] said, 'like a silver hatchet' under his spreading chesnut hair; his staccato voice and jumpy, restless manners." To Wilde he was "the most monstrous of orchids." In one of his illustrations for Pope's *The Rape of the Lock,* through the marvelous pattern of his intricately delicate line, recreating a seventeenth-century drawing room, we get a sense of flabby nastiness. The action of the picture is not of major importance, and we hardly notice the tiny scissors wielded by the gentleman on the left as he menaces the lady's elaborately coiffed hair. (Plate 130).

It is in the translation of the smooth, undetailed, flowing lines of Art Nouveau into the solid geometric shapes of architecture that we have the true transition from the conventional architectural styles of earlier periods to the architecture of the twentieth century.

Unquestionably the genius of Art Nouveau architecture was, curiously enough, a Spaniard, the Catalan, Antonio Gaudi y Cornet (1852–1926). The son of a coppersmith, Gaudi was a fervent Catalonian nationalist, and much impressed with the great Gothic structures of the Catalan past. He was also a member of the circle of Count Eusebi Güell, a rich and cultured Anglophile. In the "palace" that Gaudi designed for him in the Bohemian quarter of Barcelona (Plate 131), with its handsome parabolic entrance arches and twisting ironwork gates, through which one could see out, but not in, Güell gathered around him a brilliant circle of Barcelona's intellectuals. The house became a recognized meeting place of artists, writers, musicians (especially Wagnerians), and politicians. Güell himself was a man with wide tastes, and in his circle could be found not only an intense Catalan

131. The Güell Palace, Barcelona, designed by Antonio Gaudi y Cornet

nationalism but also an alert interest in new developments in the arts all over Europe. In this way Gaudi became acquainted with the works of Ruskin, among others. It was for his patron that Gaudi created Güell Park (Plate 132) at the turn of the century. In the marvelously imaginative stairway up to the walks of the   22.3

130. *The Rape of the Lock,* **by Aubrey Vincent Beardsley**

132. Güell Park, Barcelona, designed by Antonio Gaudi y Cornet

park, which was originally intended as a kind of garden suburb along English city-planning lines, Gaudi has used brightly colored stone as part of the main composition of the structure.

Much more than any of his houses, the Church of the Sagrada Familia (the Sacred Family) (Plate 133), stands as his most noble   225

133. Church of the Sagrada Familia, Barcelona, designed by Antonio Gaudi y Cornet

undertaking, the record of his life, for he spent forty-three years in its construction, years in which he became increasingly absorbed in his religion. The "Cathedral of the Poor," as it was popularly called, was to be a votive church built entirely from voluntary contributions, without any assistance from the Church establishment. In 1883 Gaudi took over work on it from the academic architect Villar. Although he had to follow and complete the somewhat vapid designs of that architect for the crypt, above this he was able to realize his own fantastic creation. The result was an extraordinary masterpiece along Gothic lines, but replacing Gothic detail and forms everywhere were Gaudi's own extravagant Art Nouveau motifs. His means were as extraordinary as his end results, and he even went so far as to use the discarded parts of cotton-weaving machines in the structure. Like the Gothic architects Gaudi wished to emulate, he regarded his building as almost a living thing. He allowed himself few distractions from his primary purpose, the completion of the church, at the foot of which he lived and worked in his minute workshop. There he would explain the ideas that lay behind what he was doing, for as money ran out, it became more and more necessary for Gaudi to be the spokesman and publicist for his church, as well as merely its architect. Albert Schweitzer has left a record of Gaudi at this period:

> I shall never forget how in the builders' shed near the church . . . he introduced me to his mystical theories about the proportions prevailing in the lines formed by the architecture, to reveal everywhere symbols of the divine trinity. 'This cannot be expressed (he said) in either French, German, or English, so I will explain it to you in Catalonian, and you will comprehend it, though you do not know the language . . . .

But his church remains uncompleted to this day. It was Gaudi's habit, in the early evening after finishing work, to leave his workshop and go for a walk through the streets of Barcelona. On one of these walks, crossing the street near the Sagrada Familia, he was knocked down by a streetcar and severely injured. As was his custom, he was wearing old and shabby clothes, and he was taken for a beggar. Taxis refused to carry him to the hospital. 227

Finally he was brought there, still unidentified, and placed in the paupers' ward, where he later died. A large crowd of mourners followed his funeral procession through the streets of the city to his burial place in the crypt of the Sagrada Familia.

Meanwhile, in America, great use was being made of new engineering accomplishments in the construction of taller and taller buildings. How, exactly, these were to be decorated, what known architectural form was to be applied to them, was a problem that took some decades to solve. Meanwhile various decorative motifs—classical, Gothic, Moorish, or Romanesque, all of which had enjoyed considerable revival in America—were attempted, usually either at the bottom or at the top of the increasingly tall structures. That an Art Nouveau design could be applied as well is exemplified by the top story of the Guaranty Building in Buffalo (Plate 134), designed by Louis Sullivan (1856–1924). The true solution to the problem, however, did not come until the next century.

Needless to say, the flowing lines of Art Nouveau appealed greatly to sculptors. Yet the sculptor who dominated the entire end of the nineteenth century was not a sculptor of the facile lines of Art Nouveau nor of any other previously known movement, although he attempted to adapt the ideas of impressionism to his many-faceted style.

As a child Auguste Rodin (1840–1917) showed no great aptitude for anything but drawing, with the happy result that he was sent to the École Imperiale de Dessin et de Mathématique (the Imperial School of Design and Mathematics), and later to the classes held by the stern, traditional Lecoq de Boisbaudran. This training, together with many long hours spent drawing the antique statuary in the Louvre, taught him fluency with a pencil and gave him an intimate knowledge of sculptural form. Yet, despite his obvious talent, he was continually refused admission to the École des Beaux-Arts, and this disappointment led him to doubt his artistic vocation and to consider seriously entering Holy Orders. But it soon became clear to him that the only direction in which his talents lay was sculpture. He studied in the school of the romantic Barye and, to earn money, worked for two architectural

134. The Guaranty Building, Buffalo, designed by Louis Sullivan

decorators, from whom he learned the mechanics of his craft.
And most important, he traveled to Italy, where he was much
affected by the works of Michelangelo.

The first effort that he sent to the Salon, *Man With A Broken* 229

Nose, was rejected, and for the rest of his life Rodin's works were by turns accepted by the public for his technical genius and rejected because of his constantly experimental approach. In groups like *The Kiss* (Plate 135), meant to represent the embrace of Dante's lovers, Paolo and Francesca, Rodin shows a technical perfection and finish that made him one of the few sculptors since the Renaissance who might be compared to Michelangelo himself.

Rodin's sculpture shows a technical perfection and finish that made him one of the few sculptors since the Renaissance who might be compared to Michelangelo himself. But such perfection was not always his object. At times his figures, like those of Michelangelo's later work, only partially emerge from the stone from which they are hewn, and at times, as in the case of his statue of Balzac (Plate 136), they are only roughly, if monumentally, suggested in the marble.

Rodin was fascinated by impressionist experimentation, especially in capturing the effect of movement in sculpture. In his *Walking Man* (Plate 137), the absence of the figure's arms and head makes it immediately plain that the sculptor was not interested in the exact representation of reality. What he wanted to do was to capture the impression of the movement of walking, exactly as it is seen. At the moment of the change of weight from one foot to the other, does the eye perceive only one foot on the ground or both? It was such problems that Rodin sought to solve.

Rodin's greatest undertaking was a gigantic work entitled *The Gates of Hell,* inspired by Dante's *Inferno,* which was commissioned by the Museum of Decorative Arts in Paris and on which he worked intermittently for twenty years. In the general design, Dante is seen to preside over the writhing figures of the damned. The result was a masterpiece worthy to be compared to the finest works of sculpture of the Renaissance, like Ghiberti's "Gate of Paradise" for the baptistry in Florence.

True recognition was as slow in coming to Rodin as to the impressionists, with whom he had so much in common. His statue of Balzac was rejected by the commissioning body, and not erected until many years later. Other commissioned works were refused, and some works actually mutilated by hooligans with axes. But admission of his genius came at last, and for the Paris Exhibition 231

136. *Balzac,* **by Auguste Rodin**

135. *The Kiss,* by Auguste Rodin

137. *Walking Man,* by Auguste Rodin

234

138. *Portrait of Mlle. Violette Heymann,* by Odilon Redon

139. *Silence,* **by Odilon Redon**

of 1900 the city constructed near the exhibition entrance a pavilion in which almost all his works were put on view.

The very end of the nineteenth century is marked by tremendous variety. There existed a large number of schools and movements, including followers of the greatest of the postimpressionists and also individuals working out their own concepts of what art should be, now that it was freed from the chains of the representation of visual reality. Odilon Redon (1840–1916), in his private world of strangely beautiful pastel symbolism, created pictures like his gloriously imaginative *Portrait of Mlle. Violette Heymann* (Plate 138) and his neat and economical *Silence* (Plate 139), foreshadowing the surrealists of the twentieth century. Among those who saw the first symbolist exhibition at the Café Volpini

236

140. *April,* **by Maurice Denis**

were Pierre Bonnard (1867–1947) and J. Edouard Vuillard (1868–1940), who, a decade later, banded together with Maurice Denis (1870–1943), Paul Sérusier (1865–1927), and Félix Vallotton (1865–1925) to become known as the "Nabis"—a Hebrew word meaning "Prophets." Of the five, Denis, Sérusier, and Vallotton, working in the flat patterns of color they admired in Gauguin, became inceasingly interested in Art Nouveau, resolving their forms into languid serpentine shapes. The results were canvases like Denis's poetically decorative *April* (Plate 140), Vallotton's *Moonlight* (Plate 141), and Serusier's exciting and almost completely abstract *The Bois d'Amour at Pont-Aven* (Plate 142). Bonnard and Vuillard, who shared a studio, were both attracted by the diversely patterned interiors of late-nineteenth-century 237

141. *Moonlight,* by Félix Vallotton

142. *The Bois d'Amour
at Pont-Aven,*
by Paul Sérusier

drawing rooms. In a sensitive feat of pictorial organization they contrived to unify these rooms, cluttered by objects and crowded with people and domestic pets, into charming patterns of color, as in Vuillard's *A Woman in Blue* (Plate 143) or his intimate picture of his wife, *Marie Vuillard Writing* (Plate 144), in which he created the effect of a lace curtain by scraping his paint with the sharp end of his brush handle. Bonnard managed to achieve a similar success depicting the fleeting figure of a woman in a rushing crowd in his painting *A Woman in the Street* (Plate 145).

Outside of France, the Norwegian painter, Edvard Munch (1863–1944) gave full meaning to the term "expressionism" with works like his almost unbearably intense painting entitled *The Scream* (Plate 146), and the Belgian painter, James Ensor (1860–1949) painted his technically beautiful but shocking com-

143. *A Women in Blue,* by J. Edouard Vuillard

144. *Marie Vuillard Writing*, by J. Edouard Vuillard

145. *A Woman in the Street*, by Pierre Bonnard

146. *The Scream,* **by Edvard Munch**

positions combining the grotesque images of scattered skeletons,
musical instruments, and carnival finery (see Plate 147).   In
America, Frank Lloyd Wright (1869–1959), who had worked with
Louis Sullivan, was developing a totally new style of architecture.
All these men lived well into the twentieth century, of which they
are more a part than they are of the nineteenth, just as Goya and
Blake were spiritually more a part of the nineteenth than of the
eighteenth century.   The period from 1800 to 1900 had spanned
a greater transition in the human state than any century before;
it was only fitting that in art, as in the sciences, it should have
been one of revolutionary change.

147. *Skeletons around a Stove,* by James Ensor

LIST OF ILLUSTRATIONS

1. *Coronation of Napoleon and Josephine* (detail), by Jacques Louis David. 1805–1807. The Louvre, Paris.
2. *The Gare St.-Lazare,* by Claude Monet. 1877. The Louvre, Paris.
3. *Death of Marat,* by Jacques Louis David. Royal Museum, Brussels.
4. *The Sabine Women,* by Jacques Louis David. 1799. The Louvre, Paris.
5. *Cupid and Psyche,* by Baron François Gérard. The Louvre, Paris.
6. *Pesthouse at Jaffa,* by Baron Antoine Jean Gros. 1804. The Louvre, Paris.
7. *The Battle of Nazareth,* by Baron Antoine Jean Gros. 1810. The Louvre, Paris.
8. *Portrait of the Empress Josephine,* by Pierre-Paul Prud'hon. 1805. The Louvre, Paris.
9. *The Burial of Atala,* by Anne Louis Girodet. 1808. The Louvre, Paris.
10. *Portrait of the Artist's Daughter,* by Pierre Narcisse Guérin. Museum of Fine Arts, Boulogne.
11. *Portrait of M. Fazy,* by Jacques Laurent Agasse. Museum of Art and History, Geneva.
12. *Bather of Valpinçon,* by Jean Auguste Dominique Ingres. 1808. The Louvre, Paris.
13. *Venus,* by Antonio Canova. 1812. Pitti Gallery, Florence.
14. The Arc de Triomphe, Paris, designed by Jean François Chalgrin. 1806–1835.
15. Casina Valadier, Rome, designed by Giuseppe Valadier. *c.* 1830.
16. The Glyptothek, Munich, designed by Leo von Klenze. 1816–1830.
17. Cumberland Terrace, Regent's Park, London, designed by John Nash. 1826–1827.
18. The University of Virginia, Charlottesville, designed by Thomas Jefferson. 1817–1826.
19. The Treasury Building, Washing-ton, D.C., designed by Robert Mills. 1836–1842.
20. *In a Shoreham Garden,* by Samuel Palmer. Victoria and Albert Museum, London.
21. *The Sunshade,* tapestry cartoon, by Francisco José de Goya y Lucientes. 1777. The Prado, Madrid.
22. *Self-Portrait,* by Francisco José de Goya y Lucientes. 1783. Musée Municipal, Agen, France.
23. *Family of Charles IV,* by Francisco José de Goya y Lucientes. 1800. The Prado, Madrid.
24. *Los Caprichos.* (No. 43), by Francisco José de Goya y Lucientes. 1799.
25. *The Witches Sabbath* (detail), by Francisco José de Goya y Lucientes. *c.* 1814. The Prado, Madrid.
26. *The Pilgrimage to the Miraculous Fountain of S. Isidoro,* by Francisco José de Goya y Lucientes. 1819–1820. The Prado, Madrid.
27. *The Fantastic Vision,* by Francisco José de Goya y Lucientes. 1819–1820. The Prado, Madrid.
28. *An Officer of the Chausseurs Charging,* by Jean Louis André Théodore Géricault. 1812. The Louvre, Paris.
29. *A Study of Heads of Executed Prisoners,* by Jean Louis André Théodore Géricault. 1818. The National Museum, Stockholm.
30. *The Horse Stopped by Slaves,* by Jean Louis André Théodore Géricault. 1817. The Museum of Fine Arts, Rouen.
31. *Liberty Guiding the People,* by Eugène Delacroix. 1830–1831. The Louvre, Paris.
32. *Women of Algiers,* by Eugène Delacroix. 1834. The Louvre, Paris.
33. *The Lion Hunt,* by Eugène Delacroix. 1858. Museum of Fine Arts, Boston.
34. *La Marseillaise,* by François Rude. 1833–1836. Arc de Triomphe, Paris.
35. *A Boy With a Shell Against*

245

His Ear, by Jean Baptiste Carpeaux. 1854. The Louvre, Paris.

36. *Jaguar Devouring a Crocodile,* by Antoine Louis Barye. 1938. Ny Carlsberg Glyptothek, Copenhagen.

37. *A View of Chamonix and Mont Blanc,* by Julius Schnorr von Carolsfeld. 1924. Austrian Gallery, Vienna.

38. *The Wreck of the "Hope,"* by Casper David Friedrich. 1821. Kunsthalle, Hamburg.

39. *Hell* (detail from the frescoes in the Dante room), by Joseph Anton Koch, 1822-1832. Casino Massimo, Rome.

40. *Pity,* by William Blake, *c.* 1795. Tate Gallery, London.

41. *The House of Death,* by William Blake. 1795. Tate Gallery, London.

42. *Nebuchadnezzar,* by William Blake. 1795. Tate Gallery, London.

43. *Satan Smiting Job with Sore Boils,* by William Blake. *c.* 1825. Tate Gallery, London.

44. *Newton,* by William Blake. 1795. Tate Gallery, London.

45. *The Ancient of Days,* by William Blake. 1863. Whitworth Art Gallery, Manchester.

46. *Fisherman's Cottage,* by Albert Pinkham Ryder. The Philips Collection, Washington.

47. *A Shady Pool,* by John Sell Cotman. National Gallery of Scotland, Edinburgh.

48. *The White House,* by Thomas Girtin. 1800. Tate Gallery, London.

49. *Salisbury Cathedral,* by John Constable. *c.* 1829. National Gallery, London.

50. *Cloud Study,* by John Constable. Victoria and Albert Museum, London.

51. *A View of the Stour,* by John Constable. National Gallery of Scotland, Edinburgh.

52. *A View of London from Green-*

wich, by J. M. W. Turner. Tate Gallery, London.

53. *Burning of the Houses of Parliament,* by J. M. W. Turner. 1834-1835. Museum of Art, Cleveland.

54. *Rain, Steam, and Speed—the Great Western Railway,* by J. M. W. Turner. 1844. National Gallery, London.

55. *San Benedetto, Venice,* by J. M. W. Turner, National Gallery, London.

56. *Execution of the Insurgents on the 3rd of May, 1808,* by Francisco José de Goya y Lucientes. 1814. The Prado, Madrid.

57. *A Woodland Stream,* by Constant Troyon. The Louvre, Paris.

58. *Landscape with Cows,* by Jules Dupré. The Louvre, Paris.

59. *A Windy Day,* by Pierre Étienne Théodore Rousseau. The Louvre, Paris.

60. *The Winnower,* by Jean François Millet. The Louvre, Paris.

61. *Two Peasants Going to Work,* by Jean François Millet. The Art Gallery and Museum, Glasgow.

62. *The Bridge at Narni,* by Jean Baptiste Camille Corot. 1826. National Gallery of Canada, Ottawa.

63. *View of the Colosseum,* by Jean Baptiste Camille Corot. 1825. The Louvre, Paris.

64. *A Girl Doing Her Hair,* by Jean Baptiste Camille Corot. The Louvre, Paris.

65. *The Winnowers,* by Gustave Courbet. 1854. Museum of Fine Arts, Nantes.

66. *Deer in a Forest Clearing,* by Gustave Courbet. 1866. The Louvre, Paris.

67. *The Studio* (detail), by Gustave Courbet. 1855. The Louvre, Paris.

68. *The Sea,* by Gustave Courbet. 1869. The Museum of Fine Arts, Caen.

69. *The Chess Players,* by Honoré Daumier. *c.* 1863. The Petit Palais, Paris.
70. *The Drama,* by Honoré Daumier. *c.* 1856. Neue Pinakothek, Munich.
71. *Three Peasant Women in a Village Church,* by Wilhelm Leibl. 1881. Kunsthalle, Hamburg.
72. *Croquet,* by Winslow Homer. 1866. The Art Institute, Chicago.
73. *Shadow of Death,* by William Holman Hunt. 1870–1873. City Art Gallery, Manchester.
74. *The Washing of the Feet,* by Ford Maddox Brown. Tate Gallery, London.
75. *Ophelia,* by John Everett Millais. 1852. Tate Gallery, London.
76. *Beata Beatrix,* by Dante Gabriel Rossetti. Tate Gallery, London.
77. The Houses of Parliament, London, designed by Charles Barry and A. W. N. Pugin. 1840–1850.
78. The Opéra, Paris, designed by Jean Louis Charles Garnier. 1875.
79. The Burg Theater, Vienna, designed by Gottfried Semper and Karl von Hasenanex. 1888.
80. The Hothouse, Kew Gardens, London, designed by Decimus Burton and Richard Turner. 1845–1847.
81. The National Library: Reading Room, Paris, designed by Henri Labrouste. 1862–1868.
82. *Cottages at Barbizon in the Evening,* by Charles François Daubigny. National Gallery of Scotland, Edinburgh.
83. *The Empress Eugénie Promenading on the Beach at Trouville,* by Eugène Boudin. 1863. The Art Gallery, Glasgow.
84. *Breakfast on the Grass,* by Edouard Manet. 1863. The Louvre, Paris.
85. *Monet Painting in his Floating Studio,* by Edouard Manet. 1874. Neue Pinakothek, Munich.
86. *The Bar of the Folies-Bergère,* by Edouard Manet. 1881–1882. Courtauld Institute Galleries, London.
87. *Breakfast on the Grass* (detail), by Claude Monet. 1865. The Louvre, Paris.
88. *La Grenouillère,* by Claude Monet. 1869. Metropolitan Museum, New York.
89. *The Facade of Rouen Cathedral,* by Claude Monet. 1894. The Louvre, Paris.
90. *Les Nympheas,* by Claude Monet. *c.* 1910. The Kunsthaus, Zurich.
91. *The Portrait of the Bellelli Family,* by Edgar Degas. 1859. The Louvre, Paris.
92. *The Absinthe Drinkers,* by Edgar Degas. 1876. The Louvre, Paris.
93. *The Prima Ballerina,* by Edgar Degas. 1876. The Louvre, Paris.
94. *The Café Concert: Les Ambassadeurs,* by Edgar Degas. *c.* 1877. The Museum, Lyons.
95. *The Ball at the Moulin de la Galette,* by Pierre Auguste Renoir. 1876. The Louvre Paris.
96. *A Bather,* by Pierre Auguste Renoir. The Albright Art Gallery, Buffalo.
97. *Portrait of Mme. Henriot,* by Pierre Auguste Renoir. 1877. National Gallery, Washington.
98. *The Luncheon of the Boating Party,* by Pierre Auguste Renoir. 1881. The Phillips Memorial Gallery, Washington.
99. *A Landscape with the Sea in the Distance,* by Pierre Auguste Renoir. Gallery of Modern Art, Milan.
100. *A Street in Louveciennes,* by Camille Pissarro. 1872. The Louvre, Paris.
101. *Spring at Pontoise,* by Camille Pissarro. 1877. The Louvre, Paris.

102. *Snow at Louveciennes,* by Alfred Sisley. *c.* 1874. Courtauld Institute Galleries, London.
103. *Flood at Port-Marly,* by Alfred Sisley. 1876. The Louvre, Paris.
104. *The Butterfly Hunt,* by Berthe Morisot. 1873. The Louvre, Paris.
105. *The Sisters,* by Mary Cassatt. *c.* 1885. The Art Gallery, Glasgow.
106. *Fantasy in Blue and Green,* by James Abbott McNeill Whistler. 1866. The Freer Gallery, Washington.
107. *Harmony in Gray and Green: Miss Cecily Alexander,* by James Abbott McNeill Whistler. 1872–1873. Tate Gallery, London.
108. *Bathers at Asnières,* by Georges Pierre Seurat. 1883–1884. National Gallery, London.
109. *The Circus,* by Geoges Pierre Seurat. 1891. The Louvre, Paris.
110. *St. Tropez,* By Paul Signac. 1905. Museum of the Fine Arts, Grenoble.
111. *The House of the Hanged Man at Auvers-sur-Oise,* by Paul Cézanne. 1873. The Louvre, Paris.
112. *Mont Saint-Victoire,* by Paul Cézanne. 1885–1887. The Phillips Memorial Collection, Washington.
113. *The Cardplayers,* by Paul Cézanne. Courtauld Institute Galleries, London.
114. *The Blue Vase,* by Paul Cezanne. *c.* 1885–1887. The Louvre, Paris.
115. *The Potato Eaters,* by Vincent Van Gogh. 1885. V. W. Van Gogh Collection, Laren.
116. *Sunflowers,* by Vincent Van Gogh. 1887. Metropolitan Museum, New York.
117. *Cornfield with Crows,* by Vincent Van Gogh. 1890. V. W. Van Gogh Collection, Stedelyk Museum, Amsterdam.
118. *Yellow Christ,* by Paul Gauguin. 1889. The Albright Art Gallery, Buffalo.
119. *Tahitian Girls Bearing Mango Blossoms,* by Paul Gauguin. 1899. Metropolitan Museum, New York.
120. *Siesta, Tahiti,* by Paul Gauguin. 1893. Haupt Collection, New York.
121. *Whence Do We Come? What Are We? Whither Are We Going?* by Paul Gauguin. 1897. Museum of Fine Arts, Boston.
122. *War,* by Henri Rousseau. *c.* 1894. The Louvre, Paris.
123. *The Moulin Rouge,* by Henri de Toulouse-Lautrec. 1892. The Art Institute, Chicago.
124. A Poster Announcing the Appearance of Jane Avril at the Jardin de Paris, by Henri de Toulouse-Lautrec. 1893. The Museum, Albi.
125. Glass vases, by Louis C. Tiffany. Museum of Modern Art, New York, and Arts and Crafts Museum, Hamburg.
126. *Spring,* stained-glass window, by Eugène Grasset. 1894. Museum of Decorative Arts, Paris.
127. Candlestick: the support in silver and the figure in ivory, by Frans Hoosmans. Arts and Crafts Museum, Hamburg.
128. Decorated plate, by Rene Lalique. Austrian Museum for Applied Art, Vienna.
129. Corner of a drawing room, with wool tapestry. *c.* 1900. Arts and Crafts Museum, Hamburg.
130. *The Rape of the Lock,* by Aubrey Vincent Beardsley.
131. The Guell Palace, Barcelona, designed by Antonio Gaudi y Cornet. 1885–1889.
132. Güell Park, Barcelona, designed by Antonio Gaudi y Cornet. 1900–1914.
133. Church of the Sagrada Familia, Barcelona, designed by Antonio Gaudi y Cornet. 1909–1926.

134. The Guaranty Building, Buffalo, designed by Louis Sullivan. 1894–1895.
135. *The Kiss,* by Auguste Rodin. 1898. Rodin Museum, Paris.
136. *Balzac,* by Auguste Rodin. 1897. Rodin Museum, Paris.
137. *Walking Man,* by Auguste Rodin. 1905. Rodin Museum, Paris.
138. *Portrait of Mlle. Violette Heymann,* by Odilon Redon. 1910. Museum of Art, Cleveland.
139. *Silence,* by Odilon Redon. 1911. Museum of Modern Art, New York.
140. *April,* by Maurice Denis. 1892. Kröller-Müller Museum, Otterlo.
141. *Moonlight,* by Félix Vallotton. 1895. Private collection, Milan.
142. *The Bois d'Amour at Pont-Aven,* by Paul Sérusier. 1888. Private collection, Clermont d'Oise.
143. *A Woman in Blue,* by J. Edouard Vuillard. 1890. Private collection, Paris.
144. *Marie Vuillard Writing,* by J. Edouard Vuillard. 1894. Private collection, Paris.
145. *A Woman in the Street,* by Pierre Bonnard. 1894. Private collection, Montreux.
146. *The Scream,* by Edvard Munch. 1893. National Gallery, Oslo.
147. *Skeletons around a Stove,* by James Ensor. 1889. Private collection, Fort Worth, Texas.

INDEX

Absinthe Drinkers, The (Degas), 152, 194
Academy (France), 44
Achilles, 15
Against the Grain (Huysmans), 203
Agasse, Jacques Laurent, 27
Age of Elegance, The (Bryant), 30
Ancient of Days, The (Blake), 80
An Officer of the Chausseurs Charging
    (Gericault), 56
April (Denis), 237
Arc de Triomphe (Chalgrin), 34
architects, neoclassical, 33
architecture
    Art Nouveau, 222, 228
    in the United States, 228
    neoclassical, 36, 39
artists, Greek, 15, 16
Art Nouveau, 215, 216, 220, 222, 227, 237
Athens, 15
Austen, Jane, 83

Ball at the Moulin de la Galette, The
    (Renoir), 158
Balzac (Rodin), 231
Balzac, Honore de, 68
Bar of the Folies-Bergere, The (Manet), 142
Barbizon, 100, 101, 105
Barbizon painters, 102, 105, 115, 135, 137,
    158
Barbizon School, 107, 109
Barcelona, Art Nouveau architecture,
    222
Barry, Sir Charles, 131
Barye, Antoine Louis, 67, 228
Bather, A (Renoir), 158
Bather of Valpincon (Ingres), 30, 41
Bathers at Asnieres (Seurat), 180, 181
Battle of Nazareth, The (Gros), 22
Baudelaire, 59, 111, 118
Beardsley, Aubrey Vincent, 215, 220,
    222
Beata Beatrix (Rossetti), 126
Belfort, May, 214
Bernard, Emile, 200, 202, 213
Bernhardt, Sarah, 214
Blake, William, 42, 73, 75, 77, 80, 81, 82, 83,
    112, 242
Blue Vase, The (Cezanne), 189
Bois d'Amour at Pont-Aven, The
    (Serusier), 237
Boisbaudran, Lecoq de, 228
Bonaparte, Joseph, 52
Bonnard, Pierre, 237, 239
Boucher, 105
Boudin, Eugene, 137, 144, 158
Boy with a Shell Against His Ear, A (Rude),
    63, 67
Braque, 191
Breakfast on the Grass (Manet), 138

Breakfast on the Grass (Monet), 144
Bridge at Narni, The (Corot), 107
Brown, Ford, Maddox, 126
Bruant, Aristide, 214
Brutus and His Dead Son (David), 18
Bryant, Arthur, 30
Bulfinch, Charles, 40
Burg Theatre (Semper and Hasenanex), 132
Burial of Atala, The (Girodet), 26
Burning of the houses of Parliament
    (Turner), 92
Burton, Decimus, 134
Butterfly Hunt, The (Morisot), 168
Byron, 42, 53, 69

Cafe Concert: Les Ambassadeurs, The
    (Degas), 152
Caldecott, 220
Canover, Antonio, 32
Capitol, Wash., D.C., 39, 40
Caprichos, Los (Goya), 47, 48, 49, 52, 75
Carpeaux, Jean Baptiste, 63
Casina Valadier (Valadier), 36
Casino Massimo, 73
Cassatt, Mary, 168, 173
Cezanne, Paul, 147, 180, 186, 188–192, 200
Chalgrin, Jean Francois, 34
Charles IV, 43, 44, 52
Chess Players, The (Daumier), 118
Chevreul, 137, 182
Christ in the House of His Parents
    (Millais), 126
Church of the Sagrade Familia (Gaudi), 225
Circus, The (Seurat), 182
Civil War, 135
classicism, 32, 33, 42
classicists, 69, 98, 112
Clement XV, Pope, 32
Climate of London, The (Howard), 90
Colossus, The (Goya), 47
complementary color, theory of, 136
Concert Champetre (Giorgione), 138
Constable, John, 60, 86–89, 91, 100, 101,
    107, 109, 135, 147, 167
Corneille, 17
Coronation of Napoleon and Josephine
    (David), 11, 20
Corot, Jean Baptiste Camille, 107, 109, 111,
    137, 147, 167
Cotman, John Sell, 86
Courbet, Gustave, 111–113, 122, 135, 137,
    138, 147, 151, 158, 167, 194
    President des Artistes, 115
    arrest, 115
couture, 138
Croquet (Homer), 122
cubists, 191, 192
Cumberland Terrace (Nash), 37
Cupid and Psyche, (Gerard), 22

Dante, 73, 126, 231
Darwin, 135
Daubigny, Charles Francois, 137, 140, 146
Daumier, 109, 115, 118, 138, 152, 189, 194, 214
David, Jacques Louis, 11, 16, 20–22, 26–30, 32, 41, 53, 67
Death of Marat, (David), 18
Deer in A Forest Clearing (Courbet), 112
Degas, Hilaire Germain Edgar, 147, 150–152, 168, 194, 214
de Goncourts, 98
de la Pena, Narciso Diaz, 158
Delacroix, Eugene, 29, 53, 59–63, 67–69, 87, 115, 118, 135, 146, 148
Delaroche, Paul, 105
Denis, Maurice, 202, 207, 237
Deschamps, Emile, 68
de Stael, Mme., 69
de Vigny, Alfred, 68
Dickens, Charles, 98, 126
Diderot, 67
Divine Comedy (Dante), 73
divisionism, 180, 182
Drama, The (Daumier), 118
Dumas, Alexandre, 68
Dupre, Jules, 103
Durer, 122

Early Evening (Homer), 122
Ecole des Beaux-Arts, 144, 151, 180, 212, 228
Ecole Imperiale de Dessin et de Mathe-matique, 228
Elbeuf, Prince, 14
Elgin, Earl of, 15
England, 98
Ensor, James, 239
Eve of St. Agnes, The (Keats), 129
Execution of the Insurgeants on the 3rd of May 1808 (Goya), 98
Exposition Universelle, 167
expressionism, 192, 200, 239

Family of Charles IV (Goya), 47
Fantastic Vision, The (Goya), 52
Fantasy in Blue and Green (Whistler), 173
Ferdinand VII, 52
figure painting, 158
Fisher, Archdeacon, 88
Fisherman's Cottage (Ryder), 83
Flood at Port-Marly (Sisley), 168
Fontainebleau, 101, 146, 168
Fordyce, 37, 39
France, 59, 98, 109
Franco-Prussian War, 135, 147, 167
French Revolution, 39, 91
Friedrich, Casper David, 70, 71, 72

Gainsborough, 87
Gare St. Lazare (Monet), 148
Garnier, Jean Louis Charles, 132
Gate of Paradise (Ghiberti), 231
Gates of Hell, The (Rodin), 231
Gaudi, y Cornet Antonio, 222, 224, 225, 227

Church of the Sagrada Familia, 225, 227, 228
Gaudibert, 147
Gauguin, Paul, 180, 186, 194, 197, 198, 200–203, 207, 210, 220, 237
Tahiti, 203–207, 210
Gautier, Theophile, 68, 69, 70
Gentle Art of Making Enemies, The (Whistler), 177
George IV, 27, 37
Gerard, Baron Francois, 21, 22, 30
Gericault, Jean Louis Andre Theodore, 29, 53, 56, 57, 59, 60, 67, 99, 115, 135
Germinie Lacerteux (de Goncourts), 98
Giorgione, 138, 186
Girl Doing Her Hair, A (Corot), 109
Girodet, Anne Louis, 26
Girtin, Thomas, 86, 87, 91
Gleyre, Charles Gabriel, 158, 168, 173
Glyptothek, The (Klenze), 36
Gobelins, 137
Goethe, 59, 69
Gothic Revival, 129
Gothic style, 131
Goya y Lucientes Francisco Jose de, 43, 44, 46–49, 52, 53, 62, 73, 75, 98, 99, 115, 242
Black Pictures, 52, 53
Grasset, Eugene, 220
Greek Art, 15, 16
Greenaway, Kate, 220
Gros, Baron Antoine Jean, 22, 25, 53, 67, 99
Guaranty Building (Sullivan), 228
Guell, Count Eusebi, 222
Guell Park (Gaudi), 224
Guerin, Pierre Narcisse, 27, 56, 57, 59
Guilbert, Yvette, 214
Gust of Wind (Corot), 109

Hamilton, Gavin, 32
Harmony in Gray and Green: Miss Cecily Alexander (Whistler), 173, 176
Hasenanex, Karl von, 132
Hay Wain, The (Constable), 60, 87, 100
Henriot, Mme. (Renoir), 159
Herculaneum, 14
Hercules, 15
hero cult, 42
Holbein, 122
Homer, Winslow, 122
Hoosman, Frans, 220
Horse Stopped by Slaves, The (Gericault), 59
House of Death (Blake), 77
House of the Hanged Man at Auvers-sur-Oise (Cezanne), 186
Houses of Parliament (Barry and Pugin), 131, 132
Howard, Luke, 90
Hugo, Victor, 67–70
Hunt, William Holman, 125, 126
Huysmans, 203

impressionism, 13, 41, 140, 146, 186, 187
Paris, the capitol of, 173
Whistler lawsuit, 179

impressionists, 135, 136, 140, 144, 147, 167
impressionist movement, 163
Impression: Sunrise (Monet), 147
In a Shoreham Garden (Palner), 82
industrial revolution, 126, 129
Ingres, Jean Auguste Dominique, 28–30, 32,
    40, 53, 67, 150, 151, 163, 173, 180
Inferno (Dante), 231

Jane Avril poster (Toulouse-Lautrec), 215
Jefferson, Thomas, 39
Jerusalem, 73
Josephine, Empress, 11
Jupiter and Thetis (Ingres), 28

Keats, 129
Kew Gardens, 134
Kiss, The (Rodin), 231
Klenze, Leo von, 36
Koch, Joseph Anton, 73

Labrouste, Henri, 134
Lady of The Lake (Scott), 129
Lalique, Rene, 220
landscape painting, 158
    English, 100
    French, 100
    German, 100
Landscape with a Sea in the Distance, A
    (Renoir), 163
Landscape with Cows (Dupre), 102
Lawrence, Sir Thomas, 126
Laws of Color Contrast (Chevreul), 182
Leibl, Wilhelm, 122
L'Enfant, Pierre Charles, 39
Liberty Guiding the People, (Delacroix),
    61, 63
*Lines Written from among the Euganean
    Hills* (Shelley), 95
Lion Hunt, The (Delacroix), 63
Lister, 135
Liverpool Academy, 126
Livy, 17
Louis Napoleon, 118, 138
Louis Philippe, 118
Louis XVI, 14
Louvre, Palace of, 36, 91
Lukas-bund, 72, 73
Luncheon of the Boating Party, The
    (Renoir), 159

Madrid, 98
Majas on a Balcony (Goya), 47
Mallarme, Stephane, 203
Man With A Broken Nose (Rodin), 229,
    231
Manet, Edouard, 135, 138, 140, 144, 151,
    152, 168, 194
Marie Vuillard, Writing (Vuillard), 239
Marseillaise, La (Rude), 63
Massacre at Chios (Delacroix), 87
Massimo, Marchese Carlo, 73
Mauve, Anton, 193
Michelangelo, 53, 106, 229, 231
Millais, John Everett, 125, 126
Millet, Jean Francois, 103–107, 109, 112,
    124, 181, 194

Mills, Robert, 39
Milton, John, 73, 82
Milton, May, 214
Mohammed Ali Pasha, 27
Monet, Calude, 11, 140, 144, 146–149, 152,
    158, 167, 168, 173
    nympheas pictures, 150
Mont Sainte-Victoire (Cezanne), 188, 189
Monticello, 39
Moonlight (Vallotton), 237
Morice, Charles, 203
Morisot, Berthe, 168
Morocco, 62
Mother Asking for Arms, The (Millet), 105
Moulin Rouge (Toulouse-Lautrec), 214
Munch, Edvard, 239
Munich Int'l Exhibition, 122
Murger, Henri, 70
Museum of Decorative Arts (Paris), 231

Nadar, 135, 167
Nanteuil, 70
Napoleon, 11, 16, 20–22, 29, 30, 32, 34,
    36, 52, 53, 91, 98
Napoleonic Wars, 46, 47
Nash, John, 37
National Library (Paris), 134
naturalism, 98
Nebuchadnezzar (Blake), 80
neoclassicism, 15, 30, 32, 40, 42, 53
Neptune and Nymphs (Raimondi), 138
Nobel, 135
Nobody Knows Anybody (Goya), 48
Nocturnes (Whistler), 177
Nodier, Charles, 68, 69
North Africa, 147
Northanger Abbey (Austen), 83
Notre Dame, Cathedral of, 14

Oath of the Horatii (David), 17
Oath of the Tennis Court (David), 18
Oedipus and the Sphinx, (Ingres), 28
Ophelia (Millais), 126
Orientales (Hugo), 129
Origin of Species (Darwin), 135, 136
Osuna, Countess-Dutchess of, 46
Osuna, Duke of, 44

"painter monks," 73
Palmer, Samuel, 42, 80, 82
Paradise Lost (Milton), 80, 92
Paris, 67
Paris Exhibition of 1900, 231, 236
Paris's Exposition Universelle, 112
Paris Opera, 132
Parthenon, 15
Peasant Woman Baking Bread (Millet),
    107
Peladan, 203
Pesthouse at Jaffa (Gros), 22
Phidias, 15
photography, 136
Piestre, Fernand, 212
Picasso, 191
*Pilgrimage to the Miraculous Fountain of
    S. Isidoro, The* (Goya), 52
Pinturas Negras (Goya), 52

252

Pissarro, Camille, 147, 163, 167, 168, 186, 194
Pity (Blake), 75
Poe, Edgar Allen, 82
pointillism, 180, 182, 186
pointillists, 207
Pompeii, 14, 15, 163
Portrait of M. Fazy (Agasse), 27
Portrait of Mlle. Violette Heymann (Redon), 236
postimpressionists, 180, 186, 236
Potato Eaters, The (van Gogh), 194
Poussin, 106, 187
pre-Raphaelites, 124, 125, 126
Prima Ballerina, The (Degas), 152
primitive painters, 210
Proudhon, Pierre Joseph, 111
Proust, Marcel, 140
Pugin, Augustus W.N., 131

Race of the Riderless Horse, The (Gericault), 59
Rain, Steam, and Speed (Turner), 94
Raimondi, Marc Antonio, 138
Rape of the Lock, The (Beardsley), 222
Raphael, 125, 151, 163
realism, 98, 99, 118, 124, 125, 135
Redon, Odilon, 236
Regent's Park terraces, 37
Rembrandt, 194
renaissance, 33
Renoir, Pierre Auguste, 144, 146, 147, 152, 158, 159, 163, 168, 173, 194
Revett, Nicholas, 15
Rodin, Auguste, 228
Rollin, Ledru, 105
romanticism, 40, 72, 98
romantic movement, 42, 45, 59, 67, 70, 73
romantics, 42, 45, 69, 73, 112
    English landscape painters, 86, 87
    Turner, 95
Rome, 53, 107
Roman art, 14, 15
Rosetti, Dante Gabriel, 125, 126
Rouen Cathedral (Monet), 148, 149
Rousseau, Theodore, 99, 101, 103
Rousseau, Henri, 210
Royal Academy, 87, 91, 125
Rubens, 60, 63, 158, 159
Rude, Francois, 63
Ruisdael, 87
Ruskin, John, 43, 126, 129, 176, 177, 179, 220, 224
Ryder, Albert Pinkham, 82

Sabine Women, The (David), 20
St. Jerome (Millet), 105
St. Tropez (Signac), 183
Salisbury Cathedral (Constable), 87
Salon des Refuses, 138, 173
Salon of 1870, 147
Satan Smiting Job with Sore Boils (Blake), 80
Saturn Devouring His Son (Goya), 53
Schnorr, Julius von Carolsfeld, 70, 73
Schweitzer, Albert, 227
Scott, Walter, 69, 129, 132

Scream, The (Munch), 239
sculpture, 228
Self-Portrait (Van Gogh), 196
Semper, Gottfried, 132
Sense and Sensibility (Austin), 83
Serusier, Paul, 202
Seurat, Georges Pierre, 180–182, 186, 187, 192
    divisonism, 182, 186
Shadow of Death (Hunt), 126
Shakespeare, 69
Shelley, 95
Siesta, Tahiti (Gauguin), 204
Signac, Paul, 182, 183
Silence (Redon), 236
Sisley, Alfred, 144, 147, 163, 168, 173
Sisters, The (Cassatt), 173
Sleep of Reason which Produces Monsters (Goya), 49
Snake Charmer, The (Rousseau), 210
Snow at Louveciennes (Sisley), 168
Society of French Artists, 18
Songs of Innocence (Blake), 73
Spring at Pontoise (Pissarro), 167
Stained Glass
    Art Nouveau, 216, 217
Street in Louveciennes, A (Pissarro), 167
Stuart, James, 15
Studio, The (Courbet), 112
Sullivan, Louis, 228, 242
Sunshade, The (Goya), 44
symbolic pictures, 202, 207
symbolism, 207
symbolists, 207
synthetism, 201
synthetist-symbolists, 202

Tahitian Girls Bearing Mango Blossoms (Gauguin), 204
Talleyrand, 59
Telephus, 15
Thesus, 15
Thornton, William, 40
Three Peasant Women in A Village Church (Leibl), 122
Tiffany, Louis, 216
Titian, 158
Toulouse-Lautrec, Henri de, 194, 210–212, 214, 215, 220
Transfiguration (Raphael), 125
Treasury Building, Wash. D.C. (Mills), 39
Troyon, Constant, 102, 144
Turner, Joseph Mallord, 43, 86, 91, 92, 94, 95
Turner, Richard, 134, 147
Two Peasants Going to Work (Millet), 105

University of Virginia, 39

Valadier, Giuseppe, 36
Vallotton, Felix, (Nabis), 237
van der Velde, Henry, 220
van Gogh, Theodore, 192, 193, 196
van Gogh, Vincent, 180, 186, 192–194, 196–200, 213
    impressionism, 192
    expressionism, 192

253

Velasquez, 62
Venus (Canover), 32
Vergil, 82
Verhaeren, 182
Veronese, 186, 192
Versuvius, 14
View of Chamonix and Mont Blanc
 (Schnorr), 70
View of London from Greenwich, A
 (Turner), 92
View of the Colosseum (Corot), 107
View of the Stour, The (Constable), 90
Villar, 227
Vuillard, J. Edouard, 237

Walking Man (Rodin), 231
Walter, Thomas, 40
War (Rousseau), 210, 211
Washing of the Feet (Brown), 126
Washington, D.C., 39
Watteau, 105
Whence Do We Come? What Are We?
 Whither Are We Going? (Gauguin),
 204, 206, 207

Whistler, James Abbott McNeill, 146, 173,
 176, 177
White House, The (Girtin), 86
Wilde, Oscar, 215, 222
Winckelmann, Johann J., 15, 16, 17
Windy Day, A (Rousseau), 103
Winnower, The (Millet), 105, 112
witchcraft, 52
Witches Sabbath, The (Goya), 52
Woman in Blue, A (Vuillard), 239
Woman in the Street, A (Bonnard), 239
Women of Algiers (Delacroix), 63
Woodland Stream, A (Troyan), 101,
 102
Wordsworth, 43, 104
Workman's Monday, The (Millet), 105
Wreck of the "Hope", The (Friedrich),
 71
Wright, Frank Lloyd, 242

Yellow Christ (Gauguin), 201

Zola, Emile, 98, 186, 189